THE GREAT EXPEDITION

Sir Francis Drake on the Spanish Main 1585–86

ANGUS KONSTAM

First published in Great Britain in 2011 by Osprey Publishing,
Midland House, West Way, Botley, Oxford, OX2 0PH, UK
44–02 23rd St, Suite 219, Long Island City, NY 11101, USA

E-mail: info@ospreypublishing.com

A CIP catalogue record for this book is available from the British Library

Print ISBN: 978 1 84908 245 7
PDF e-book ISBN: 978 1 84908 246 4

Page layout by Bounford.com, Cambridge, UK
Index by Mike Parkin
Typeset in Sabon
Maps by Bounford.com, Cambridge, UK
3D BEVs by Alan Gilliland
Originated by United Graphic Pte, Singapore
Printed in China through Worldprint

11 12 13 14 15   10 9 8 7 6 5 4 3 2 1

Osprey Publishing is supporting the Woodland Trust, the UK's leading
woodland conservation charity, by funding the dedication of trees.

www.ospreypublishing.com

EDITOR'S NOTE

For ease of comparison between types, Imperial/American
measurements are used almost exclusively throughout this book.
The following data will help in converting the Imperial/American
measurements to metric:

1 mile = 1.6km

1lb = 0.45kg

1yd = 0.9m

1ft = 0.3m

1in = 2.54cm/25.4mm

1gal = 4.5 litres

1 ton (US) = 0.9 tonnes

CONTENTS

INTRODUCTION

Sir Francis Drake is probably one of the most famous figures of the 16th century – a man of action who came to symbolize Elizabethan England just as much as the Queen he served. Drake was the archetypal Elizabethan 'Sea Dog'. He was the leading member of that unique band of seafarers who helped thwart the Spanish Armada, but who also pursued their own destiny as explorers, pirates and adventurers. Drake himself has been described as a privateer, a courtier, a politician, a slave trader, an explorer, a naval commander and, of course, as a pirate. Clearly Francis Drake was a man of many parts.

To the English, Drake was a hero and one of the greatest seamen of his age. To the Spanish, though, he was *El Draque* (The Drake), a name whose similarity to the Latin *draco* (dragon) was used by Catholic propagandists to vilify him as a creature of evil. At best his enemies saw him as a pirate, operating beyond the bounds of legal and civil niceties. The real Drake lay somewhere in between these polarized views, a complex character whose exploits thrilled and horrified in equal measure. Without doubt Drake was a gifted leader of men, a skilled navigator and sailor, and an accomplished naval tactician. He was also driven by a burning religious zeal, and a voracious appetite for plunder.

This book describes his greatest raid – his assault on the Spanish Main in the mid 1580s, an action that served as a catalyst for war. By that time, however, he had nothing to prove. He was already a national hero, and the darling of the Elizabethan court. He had just been knighted by his sovereign, and the plunder from his recent raid into the Pacific had made him the equivalent of a multi-millionaire. What drove him to launch this new and powerful expedition was a passionate desire for revenge, staunch loyalty to his Queen and, above all, his insatiable desire for wealth.

By placing the greatest seaman of the age in command of the largest naval raid England had ever mounted against the Spanish Main, Queen Elizabeth was playing a game of global brinkmanship. Failure could lose her the kingdom, and her life. The stakes had never been higher. Once Drake set sail there would be no turning back. The Queen also had much to gain. War against Spain was looming, and to wage it King Philip II would need money – lots of it. His biggest source of revenue lay in the New World, in the silver mines of Peru and Mexico, the gold mines of Colombia and the emerald fields of Venezuela. Every year a portion of these great riches was taken to the ports of the Spanish Main, where they were shipped to Spain in well-protected treasure fleets. Queen Elizabeth hoped that by capturing the ports she could capture the treasure. Thus she could fill her own coffers while denying her Spanish rival the money he needed to strike back. It was audacious, bold and, at least in diplomatic terms, a wildly reckless gambit but then by 1585 Elizabeth and her advisors were running out of options.

Historians have often portrayed the raid as a pre-emptive strike – an attempt to launch a crippling blow against the Spanish before the inevitable start of hostilities. This view makes the mistake of viewing things with the benefit of hindsight. In fact, Elizabeth and her advisors saw Drake's expedition as a last great chance for peace, a drastic form of diplomatic coercion designed to avoid conflict, rather than to start it. As we shall see, the raid was originally meant to be a very different affair,

FRANCISCVS DRAECK · NOBILISSIMVS EQVES ANGLIAE · IS EST QVI TOTO T TERRARVM ORBE CRCMDVGO

jd circūmducto pernosc in longitudine, in latitud ne est Jmpossibile, etc:

Sir Francis Drake (c. 1540–96), seen in the three-quarter length armour he wore during his land operations on the Spanish Main. The Latin inscription in this contemporary engraving rather flatteringly describes him as 'England's most noble knight', and the circumnavigator of the globe.

launched against a target half a world away from the Caribbean. It also came within a hair's breadth of being called off, as Elizabeth began to have second thoughts. Ever the opportunist, Drake solved the Queen's problem by sailing anyway, before Elizabeth could change her mind.

What followed became the stuff of legend, a dramatic stab against the very heart of Spain's overseas empire. Drake was in his element, and this proved to be his finest hour. His earlier forays into the Caribbean had been mere pinpricks. This was a rapier thrust. His foray into the Pacific earned him a fortune in plunder, but this raid was on a different scale entirely. Rather than commanding a single ship, Drake led a whole invasion force, ready and willing to cause as much destruction as they could, and his men were eager for treasure. After all, like all raids of this kind this was as much a business speculation as a military adventure, and with the Queen as his main financial backer, Drake not only had to strike hard against the Spanish, but he also had to turn a profit. This then, would be the wily Sea Dog's greatest test.

THE FORMING OF DRAKE

Of all the Elizabethan Sea Dogs, Drake was the perfect choice as commander of this great expedition. He was resourceful, aggressive, and he knew the Caribbean like no other Englishman of his generation. Better still, he had a deep-rooted dislike of the Spanish, a legacy of his experience at their hands at San Juan de Ulúa 17 years before. He could be relied upon to inflict as much damage on Spain's overseas empire as he could. Besides, as this was a royally sanctioned quest for treasure, Drake's avarice meant that he would make a thorough job of plundering the riches of the Spanish Main, on behalf of his Queen and his other backers. It can even be said that Drake's experiences had groomed him for this command – the expedition would be the culmination of almost two decades of seafaring, privateering and warfare.

Francis Drake was born in Tavistock, a small market town on the western edge of Dartmoor, some 15 miles north of Plymouth. He was the eldest son of Edmund and Mary Drake, a young farming couple whose lands at Crowndale on the banks of the River Tavy were rented from the local landowner Lord Russell, the Earl of Bedford. Actually, Edmund's elder brother John ran the farm; his younger brother merely assisted him. Clearly the Drakes had good social connections – Francis was named after his godfather Francis Russell, the teenage son of the local landowner.

The exact year of Francis' birth is unclear, but it probably took place around 1539 or 1540. He was the eldest of 12 brothers, but what could have been an idyllic rural childhood was cut short in 1549 when Francis and the family fled the country. Edmund Drake was a staunch Protestant, and was caught up in the local religious unrest dubbed the 'Prayerbook Rebellion'. The family escaped to Kent, where they established a new home in a houseboat (or hulk), moored in the River Medway. Edmund re-invented himself as a Protestant clergyman, preaching to local seafarers.

In his early teens Francis went to sea as a crewman of a trading vessel, plying between Kent and nearby European ports. He probably served as an apprentice to the owner, as it appears he inherited the vessel and the business when his mentor died. This meant that by the time he was 20 Drake was already an experienced seaman, and his own master.

Still, it seems the young man preferred blue water sailing to coastal trade, as he sold his vessel in Plymouth, and drew on his family connections to join the employ of his second cousin John Hawkins. By that time Hawkins had already made one successful trading voyage to the Caribbean, selling slaves he picked up on the West African coast to colonists in the Spanish New World. In 1564–65 Hawkins repeated the voyage, but the indications are that Drake didn't accompany him. Instead he acted as Hawkins' representative on a trading voyage to Spain and back. His big chance would come on Hawkins' third Caribbean voyage. The only problem was that what Hawkins was doing was illegal, or more accurately it was illegal in the eyes of the Spanish.

The Spaniards had a proprietary attitude to the New World in general and the Caribbean in particular. While other Europeans had occasionally ventured into these waters – the first English 'interloper' did so in 1527 – the region was generally seen as off-limits. In the Treaty of Tordesillas (1494), drawn up in the wake of Columbus' first voyage, Spain was granted control of all lands to the west of a line of longitude 38° West, which bisected the Atlantic Ocean, leaving Brazil to the Portuguese and the rest of the Americas to the Spanish.

Until 1558 English ventures 'beyond the line' were discouraged, for fear of sparking a diplomatic incident. The accession of Queen Elizabeth I that year marked a change of policy, and the Spanish Main was no longer barred to English adventurers.

John Hawkins was quick to take advantage of this development. However, he sailed across the line with peaceful intentions, coming to trade rather than to plunder. In 1562 he sailed from Plymouth in three small ships, and on the West African coast he visited local chieftains, where he exchanged trade goods for slaves. He then transported 300 of these unfortunates across the Atlantic, and arrived in the West Indies early the following year. Hawkins headed to Hispaniola, but he avoided the main settlement of Santo Domingo, and instead he anchored further down the coast, where he sold his slaves to local plantation owners. He returned to England a wealthy man.

Hawkins' second voyage in 1564 was a much larger affair, as he had secured several important backers. These included Queen Elizabeth herself, who leased Hawkins the ageing royal warship *Jesus of Lubeck* as part of her stake. Once again Hawkins collected a cargo of slaves on the West African

John Hawkins (1532–95) was a kinsman of Drake, and one of the leading shipowners in Plymouth. Drake accompanied Hawkins on his trading voyage to the Spanish Main in 1567–69, and both men escaped the debacle at San Juan de Ulúa.

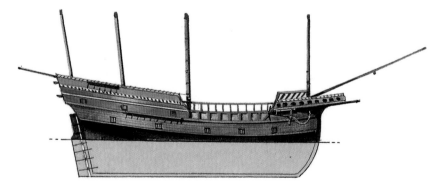

When Queen Elizabeth leased John Hawkins the ageing warship *Jesus of Lubeck* in 1564, the Plymouth adventurer set about modernizing her, lowering her superstructure and making her more seaworthy. Her new appearance is shown below – this was how she looked when she was captured by the Spanish at San Juan de Ulúa in 1568. Painting by Tony Bryan. (Originally in Osprey New Vanguard 149: Tudor Warships (2).)

coast, but this time when he reached the West Indies he sailed southwards towards the Tierra Firme – the Caribbean coast of South America. The Spanish settlers of Margarita were unwilling to do business with him, for fear of reprisal from the Spanish authorities. Hawkins finally managed to sell his slaves in Rio de la Hatcha further up the coast, but only after he threatened to turn his guns on the town. This threat, though, was almost certainly a pre-arranged gesture, arranged between Hawkins and the town mayor as a means of saving face, and to avoid official retribution. In late 1565, Hawkins returned to Plymouth, his voyage having proved even more lucrative than the last. Drake must have envied his kinsman, and he was determined not to miss out on any new opportunity.

First, however, Drake would sail under a different commander. The political repercussions of Hawkins' last foray into the Spanish Main kept Hawkins himself in England, so when a new expedition left Plymouth on 9 November 1566, the three small ships were led by John Lovell, a captain in Hawkins' employ. This time Drake went with them, venturing further from England than he ever had before. Off the Cape Verde Islands Lovell attacked and captured several Portuguese ships, which gave Drake his first experience of naval combat. This action was nothing other than piracy, but Lovell realized that the niceties of European law and diplomacy counted for little in African or American waters. The likelihood is that these attacks gave Lovell all the slaves he needed, saving him the need to spend several unhealthy weeks on the African coast.

After a fast transatlantic voyage, Lovell arrived off the small settlement of Borburata, on the coast of Tierra Firme (now Venezuela), where he encountered a similar squadron of French interlopers. Lovell moved along the coast to Rio de la Hatcha, where the local administrator refused to deal with him. Lovell lingered for a week, hoping for a change of heart that never came. He then sailed off, pausing only to deposit the least healthy of his slaves on the beach. He may well have sold the rest of his human cargo on Hispaniola, but by September 1567 Lovell and Drake were back in Plymouth.

There Drake discovered that Hawkins was making his final preparations for another trading voyage, and volunteered his services. This time Drake would be part of it, serving Hawkins as one of his junior officers. Hawkins' squadron consisted of five ships, two of which were leased to him by the Queen. The venerable royal warship *Jesus of Lubeck* of 700 tons had been modified extensively, but she was still old, slow and barely seaworthy. The smaller 300-ton royal warship *Minion* was better suited to the voyage, but regardless Hawkins needed the Queen's backing, and was in no position to reject her stake in the venture. The rest of his force consisted of the smaller ships *William and John* and *Swallow*, accompanied by the smaller *Judith* (a 50-ton bark). Finally these five ships were accompanied by the pinnace *Angel*, a tiny vessel of just 35 tons.

The expedition sailed from Plymouth on 2 October 1567, with Hawkins flying his flag from the *Jesus of Lubeck*. The voyage seemed doomed from the start. A storm forced Hawkins to take shelter in Tenerife, and the Spanish governor duly wrote to Madrid, warning them that Hawkins was undoubtedly bound for the Spanish Main. When Hawkins eventually arrived off the West African coast he found that the coastal tribes were

An English seaman of the late 16th century, a detail from the frontispiece of *The Mariners Mirrour* by the Dutch pilot Lucas Jansz Waghenaer, and engraved by Theodore de Bry. His dress is typical of the well-dressed maritime officer of this period.

Queen Elizabeth I (1533–1603, reigned from 1558) used Drake as a strategic weapon, in an attempt to encourage King Philip II of Spain to negotiate with her, rather than to embark on a costly war with England.

unwilling to trade with him. He resorted to Lowell's method of overpowering Portuguese slave ships, and taking their human cargo. Drake was rewarded with the command of one of these captured vessels – the *Gratia Dei*. Actually, it had only just been captured from the Portuguese by the French, but Hawkins and Drake cared little about rightful ownership.

The expedition was still short of slaves, so Hawkins decided to involve himself in African politics. A coastal tribe was at war with an inland one, so the Englishman offered his services in return for a share of the prisoners. In January Hawkins led an attack on a fortified village on the River Tagarin, in what is now Liberia. English firepower proved decisive, and Hawkins duly secured another 250 slaves. The expedition then set sail for the Americas, making landfall off Dominica in late March 1568. His first port of call was the Isla Margarita off the Tierra Firme coast, but the governor refused to trade with him. He encountered the same response at Borburata, Curaçao and Rio de la Hatcha. In fact, at the last port the Spanish even fired on Hawkins' ships, driving Hawkins back out to sea.

He eventually appeared off Santa Marta, where the residents proved a little more forthcoming. He went through the same ritual he performed off Rio de la Hatcha three years before, pretending to fire on the tiny settlement to induce its surrender. This display then gave the governor no option but to trade with the interlopers. Hawkins managed to sell 110 slaves there, and set off westwards in search of another marketplace. The gun batteries of Cartagena opened fire when he approached, but the English lingered just out of range for several days before heading away to the north. Drake undoubtedly used this time to study the defences of the port. Hawkins' force now consisted of eight vessels – his original flotilla, the *Gratia Dei* and another Portuguese prize.

By mid August they were passing through the Yucatan Channel, the start of a voyage around Cuba and out into the Atlantic. However, they were overtaken by a violent storm – probably a hurricane – and the fleet was blown deep into the Gulf of Mexico. The *William and John* became separated from the rest, and returned to Plymouth. The remainder of the squadron stayed together, but the ageing *Jesus of Lubeck* almost foundered, as 'on both sides of her stern the planks did open and shut with every sea'. If his flagship was going to make it back home Hawkins needed to put into a port to repair her. He settled on Vera Cruz on the coast of Mexico, an important treasure port and a thriving town.

The town was defended by an island fort – San Juan de Ulúa – which Hawkins captured by bluff, by pretending his squadron was a Spanish one in need of repair. He then moored his ships under the guns of the fortress, and his men set to repairing their ships. Hawkins was in a hurry. Local officials told him that the annual treasure *flota* (fleet) was due to arrive at the end of the month, and he wanted to be far offshore when it appeared. Unfortunately for him, on 14 September – just two days later – the *flota* arrived, and Hawkins was trapped. The Spanish naval commander Admiral Luján, realized that a straightforward battle would be costly, so he and

The port of Vera Cruz in Mexico was an important Spanish treasure port during this period, and consequently the island of San Juan de Ulúa, which lay just off the harbour, was heavily fortified. It was here that Hawkins and Drake were driven by a hurricane in 1568.

les Isles de St. Jean du Luz

la Forteresse de St Jean du Luz ou l'on amare les Vaisseaux

le Mole

la Douane la Maison du Gouverment

Vera Cruz a Mexico

Hawkins arranged a truce. While his intentions were probably pure, his passenger Don Martinez Enriques, the new Viceroy of Mexico, had no intention of dealing with interlopers. While both sides watched each other warily, the Viceroy ordered the admiral to prepare a surprise attack.

At dawn on 23 September the Spanish launched their assault, overwhelming the small English garrison guarding the fortress. They then turned the guns on the English ships moored in front of them, while the Spanish galleons joined in the bombardment. The *Jesus of Lubeck* attracted most of the fire, and within an hour she was battered, dismasted and holed. Hawkins had little choice but to abandon her, and concentrated on saving his remaining ships and their crews. As the *Minion* manoeuvred to pick up the flagship's crew, a Spanish fireship appeared, prompting Captain Hampton of the *Minion* to veer away as the last of the *Jesus'* crew were clambering to safety. Hawkins jumped for it, but others weren't so lucky, and were left behind to be captured by the Spaniards. In fact, only two English ships made it to safety – the battered *Minion* and the smaller *Judith*, which was now commanded by Francis Drake.

The two ships became separated in the dark, and by dawn the *Minion* was alone. Drake was already over the horizon, leaving his kinsman to fend for himself. Hawkins clearly thought Drake had deserted him, and when the *Minion* finally limped home in late January 1569 he said as much. Drake himself arrived in Plymouth less than a week earlier, and of more than 300 men of both ships who escaped the debacle at San Juan de Ulúa, only 25 survived long enough to see England again. Others who insisted on being put ashore rather than face starvation at sea were butchered by local Indians. Few of those left behind in Vera Cruz ever returned home either. Instead they ended their days as galley slaves, or were burned as heretics.

Neither Drake nor Hawkins ever forgave the Spaniards for their treachery. Hawkins wrote to the Queen seeking redress, as according to English law he could be issued with a 'letter of reprisal', which allowed him to confiscate Spanish goods to help recoup his losses. The fact that he was in Spanish waters illegally was never mentioned. However, it was Drake rather than Hawkins who would return to the Caribbean to seek revenge. Before San Juan de Ulúa, Drake had a strong dislike of the Spanish because their religious beliefs were at odds with his. What he viewed as the treachery of the Spanish Viceroy turned this dislike into a consuming hatred, and the desire to avenge his lost shipmates. Drake would soon prove that the Spanish had tangled with the wrong man.

DRAKE'S WAR

First though, Drake had to attend to some private business. For a year or more he had been courting a lady called Mary Newman, and on 4 July 1569 they were married in a church in Plymouth. We know very little about Drake's activities over the months that followed, so presumably he was making the most of his new-found domestic bliss in Plymouth. He also spent the time arranging a voyage of reprisal against the Spanish. Drake lacked

Early English raids in the Caribbean.

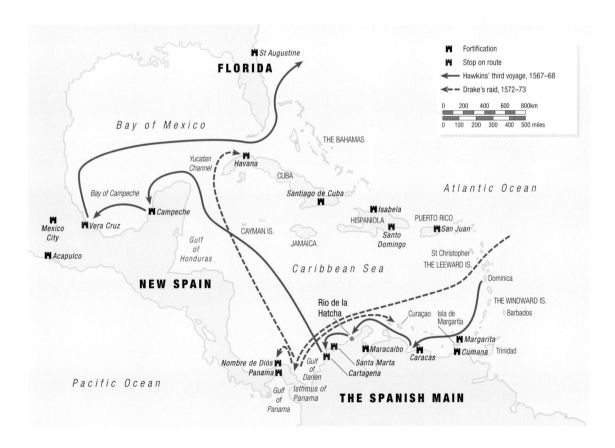

The English ships used by Drake and his contemporaries ranged from large royal warships to tiny pinnaces. Although slightly fanciful, this depiction of the 450-ton *Golden Lion* gives us a fair impression of what the larger of these vessels looked like.

Hawkins' money and connections, but although he was a relatively young and unknown commander, he managed to gather together a small force. Still, it was barely large enough to count as a fully fledged squadron, let alone one capable of causing trouble in American waters. Therefore Drake's expedition of 1569–70 could be little more than a reconnaissance in force.

His own flagship was the *Dragon*, a tiny 35-ton vessel, little bigger than a large modern sailing yacht. It was accompanied by the 25-ton vessel *Swan* of Plymouth, a vessel Drake bought from the proceeds of his earlier voyage with Lovell. The total crew of both ships couldn't have been more than 50 men. Like most privateers they weren't paid – instead they expected a share of any plunder, so like their commander they were eager for Spanish treasure. The small expedition set sail in November 1569, and presumably Drake made landfall in the West Indies early the following year. Unfortunately we know little about his activities on this first independent voyage. The Spanish reported several interlopers were operating in the Caribbean that year, most of whom were French. One of them was Drake.

Drake returned to Plymouth in the early summer of 1570. Queen Elizabeth subsequently granted Drake his letter of reprisal, giving him the legal right to attack Spanish ships and settlements. She presented one to Hawkins as well, but he was also given a royal appointment as a naval administrator, in charge of the Royal Dockyard at Deptford on the River

Thames. His new job would keep him busy for several years, which meant he was unable to take advantage of his licence to wage a private war. This meant that of the two captains, it was Drake who would return to the Spanish Main, eager for revenge.

Drake immediately began organizing a new and larger expedition. This activity in itself suggests that his previous reconnaissance proved fruitful; without even a little plunder he would have been hard-pressed to raise another volunteer crew. This time the expedition would be even smaller, as Drake only used one ship – the little *Swan*. He probably sailed in November or December, as by mid February 1571 Drake appeared off the Isthmus of Panama. On 21 February he encountered a small Spanish warship near the mouth of the River Chagres. Drake and his men took it by surprise, boarding it before the Spanish had a chance to defend themselves. This would be the first of several prizes. As the Spanish described it: 'upon the coast of Nombre de Dios [Drake] did rob diverse barques in the river of Chagres, and in the same river did rob diverse barques that were transporting of merchandise.' Drake might only have had one small ship, but he knew how to cause trouble.

By that time he also had allies. French pirates (or 'corsairs' as they preferred to be called) were operating in the same area, and Drake fell in with a French Huguenot (French Protestant) captain, possibly the Jean Bontemps who was killed later that year during a botched attack on the Spanish island of Curaçao. The two interlopers must have operated together, as Drake's small crew would have found it difficult to plunder so many ships without help. The Spanish themselves put the value of the plunder at 40,000 ducats, a sizeable fortune comprised of gold, silver and – according to the Spanish – 'silks and taffeta'. Drake returned to Plymouth a rich man.

The Nombre de Dios raid

Drake began planning his next venture almost as soon as he returned. Once again he used his brother John Drake's diminutive *Swan* of Plymouth, but this time he was flew his flag in the larger *Pasco* (or *Pasha*) of 70 tons, a vessel which was almost certainly supplied by John Hawkins, who was one of Drake's financial backers. They two ships carried 73 men and boys between them. The expedition sailed in March 1572, and by July Drake was back in his old hunting ground of the Isthmus of Panama. This time, though, he had a very specific objective. He planned to attack Nombre de Dios, reportedly the treasure house of the New World.

During the later 16th century, the bulk of Spanish wealth from the New World came from the silver mines of Peru, the largest of which – Potosi – produced more silver each year than all the other mines put together in Europe or the Americas. Every year a fifth of the silver produced in these mines was earmarked for the Spanish treasury, and it was shipped northwards up the Pacific coast to Panama. From there it was transported across the Isthmus to Nombre de Dios, where it was stored, ready for collection by the annual Spanish treasure *flota*. Drake hoped to capture this huge cargo of silver before the Spanish ships arrived.

The treasure port of Nombre de Dios on the Caribbean coast of the Isthmus of Panama, as depicted in a crude Spanish chart of the harbour, drawn in 1541. Drake unsuccessfully attacked the small port in the summer of 1572.

First, however, he needed a base. He soon found what he was looking for – a half-hidden inlet about 130 miles south-east of Nombre de Dios, which he called Port Pheasant. Although its exact location was never revealed, it was probably the inlet near Darien, which was later called Puerto Escoces, as it became the site of a doomed Scottish colony in the last two years of the 17th century. Drake used his time in the anchorage to take on water and stores, to organize his men for the raid and to plan the attack. It was in Port Pheasant that Drake was joined by a small English ship, commanded by another interloper, Captain James Raunce. Raunce was the former master of the *William and John*, which took part in Hawkins' last voyage but which avoided the debacle at San Juan de Ulúa. His vessel added another 50 men to Drake's force.

Drake then sailed up the coast, and on the afternoon of 28 July he dropped anchor a few miles below the treasure port. Captain Raunce was left behind to guard the three ships, while Drake embarked 73 of his men in four small specially built pinnaces, and sailed them to within a mile or so of the town. He planned to launch a night attack on an unsuspecting port, and with the advantage of surprise on his side he had every chance of success. However, a Spanish vessel anchored close to the port spotted the English pinnaces, and a boat was launched to raise the alarm. Fortunately for Drake, one of his pinnaces blocked its path, and the Spanish longboat veered away. In fact, Drake's dawn attack achieved complete surprise. The assault carried the English raiders into the centre of the town. Their big advantage was that the enemy had no idea just how few attackers there were. That was when it all started to go wrong.

Drake had some difficulty keeping his men together as they ran through the buildings in search of plunder. They encountered the town's *alcalde* (mayor) in the main square, where the town militia were gathering. A short firefight ensued, but Drake's men had the better of the exchange, and the defenders soon broke and ran. The English now controlled the town. At that moment a tropical downpour broke, soaking Drake's men and wetting their powder and bowstrings. They took shelter as best they could, but the storm lasted more than half an hour, which gave the defenders a chance to rally. This time the Spanish realized they had numbers on their side.

Unknown to his men, Drake had been wounded in the fight, and he was losing blood. When the storm passed, he led his men to the main royal treasure warehouse, and ordered his brother John Drake to break down the door. It was then that Drake passed out through loss of blood, leaving his

Although this coloured engraving depicts a French Huguenot raid on a Spanish port in the Caribbean, rather than one led by Drake, the scene shows how these raids were carried out – an amphibious landing, a quick assault, then the looting and destruction of the town.

men virtually leaderless. John bound his leg, and the English commander was carried back to the boats, followed by the rest of his men. The treasure house remained untouched as the attackers concentrated on saving their leader. The opportunity had gone, the Spanish re-occupied the town centre and there was nothing for the attackers to do but row away to safety.

Drake's first major attack on the Spanish Main was a complete failure. Actually, Drake might have been luckier than he imagined. The Spanish treasure fleet had already cleared out the contents of the warehouse a few weeks earlier, and discovering it to be empty would have seriously weakened his credibility with his men. James Raunce decided to cut his losses and sail for home, leaving while Drake was still convalescing. Drake, though, was made of sterner stuff. He decided his men needed a quick success to boost their flagging morale, so he decided to sail south to Cartagena, his two small ships towing three pinnaces behind them.

The inner port was too well protected to assault, but Drake managed to slip into the outer roads undetected, and fell upon the nearest Spanish ship. It held nothing of value, nor did another larger 250-ton vessel. It turned out that the Spanish had warning of Drake's approach, and all the valuable ships that could do so sought refuge behind the protective guns covering the inner harbour. Drake had been thwarted again, although the Spanish were also unable to prevent him from pillaging the two ships within sight of the town. He withdrew to the Islas San Bernardo, just off the coast. He really didn't have enough crew to man all his ships, so he scuttled and burned the *Swan*, which left him with just the *Pasco*, the three pinnaces and about 60 men. It was hardly a major force, but Drake was determined to make his mark. He returned to Cartagena, but once again he found nothing of much value to plunder. He continued eastwards as far as Curaçao, but despite capturing a few prizes he never found a target of any real worth.

Meanwhile, Drake left his brother John in the islands with the third pinnace, with orders to gather supplies by trading with the local Indians, and to establish contact with the Cimaroons (runaway slaves) who inhabited the Darien coast. At Nombre de Dios the English had been joined by one of them, a former slave known as Diego. Drake soon realized that these desperate men hated the Spanish as much as he did. That made them potentially useful allies. Drake's plan was to use this local contact to help him ambush the Spanish silver shipment before it reached Nombre de Dios, during its transit across the Isthmus of Panama. Unfortunately, John Drake was killed while attacking a passing Spanish ship, so when his brother Francis returned he not only had to deal with a double personal tragedy – a younger brother also succumbed to disease – but he discovered from the Cimaroons that his new plan had a flaw.

It was now December 1572. The next shipment was scheduled to take place in just a few weeks, and Drake had very little time to move his force to the Isthmus, put his men into place and set up an ambush before the Spanish treasure reached the safety of Nombre de Dios. It was a race against time. It took two weeks of marching before Drake and his small force reached their ambush site, a few miles from the village of Vente Cruces, and some 18 miles from Panama.

By mid February 1573, Drake had won his race. He had just 18 sailors with him, accompanied by around 20 Cimaroon allies. The Spanish would be using the Camino Real (Royal Road) that crossed the Isthmus from Panama to Nombre de Dios, and Drake hoped that by ambushing them close to the start they would be more likely to be off-guard. He split his men into two groups – one on each side of the road – and took the precaution of making them wear their shirts over their clothing, to help distinguish friend from foe.

Cimaroon lookouts alerted Drake when the Spanish approached, and soon the waiting Englishmen could hear the bells worn by the silver-carrying pack mules. Then, just moments before the silver train appear, a lone Spanish horseman rode into view, riding in the opposite direction (from Nombre de Dios). At that moment one of the English seamen, Robert Pike, rose from the bushes, wearing his discoloured white shirt. He had been drinking, and whether he chose the wrong moment to relieve himself or he was simply too befuddled to know what he was doing is unclear. In any event he was spotted, and the rider galloped off down the road to warn the approaching silver

In this late 16th-century chart showing the Isthmus of Panama, north is at the bottom, and the town of Porto Bello on the Mar del Norte lies on the Caribbean coast, a few miles west of Nombre de Dios.

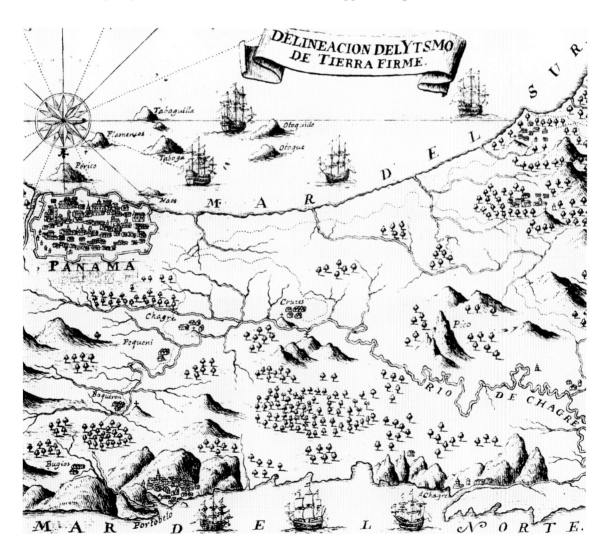

19

train. The treasure convoy was immediately turned around, and was protected by its strong escort as it withdrew back down the road towards Panama. Drake had little option but to make his escape, no doubt cursing Robert Pike as he went. Weeks of effort had been wasted by one drunken seaman.

The raiders passed through the village of Vente Cruces as they withdrew, driving out a small Spanish garrison before looting the place of provisions and a meagre haul of valuables. Drake then withdrew back to the coast and his ships, well aware that the countryside would soon be swarming with Spanish troops. They reached safety on 23 February, and Drake immediately began planning a second attempt. This time, though, he had more men at his command. On 23 March he was joined by a French Huguenot interloper called Guillaume Le Testu, and they decided to make a joint attempt at intercepting the silver shipment, which was due to leave Panama in a few weeks. One suspects that this time Robert Pike was left on board the ships.

During the last week of March, a force of 20 Frenchmen, 15 Englishmen and 20 Cimaroons landed on the coast a few miles from Nombre de Dios, and this time Drake set up his ambush on the outskirts of the port, so close

The Spanish used the local population to extract silver for them from the mines in Mexico and Peru, as shown in this engraving by Theodore de Bry. The Spanish crown came to rely on this treasure to fund its wars in Europe.

that his scouts could hear the sound of carpenters repairing the waiting treasure galleons. This time there was no blunder. On 31 March the Spanish silver train appeared, and the plan worked perfectly. After a brief fight the 45-man escort were driven off, but a Cimaroon was killed in the exchange and Le Testu mortally wounded. While Drake and his men set about looting what they could from the pack mules, Le Testu's men made arrangements to carry their dying commander to safety. In the end the plunder – reputedly valued at 200,000 'pieces-of-eight' (pesos) – was too much to carry, and the Spanish in Nombre de Dios were expected to appear any minute. Drake took what little he could and buried the rest, hoping to come back for it later. With the Spanish now in full pursuit, the gravely wounded Le Testu had to be left behind too, and he was executed by the vengeful Spaniards.

Three days later Drake reached the site where he expected his pinnaces to be waiting for him. They weren't there – a storm had delayed them. Ever resourceful, Drake built a raft, and it carried them down the Francisco River to safety, where the raiders finally came upon the pinnaces, working their way upriver to meet him. It would have been a joyful reunion if he had more plunder to show for his efforts. However, Drake had managed to seize enough gold to turn what had been a disastrous voyage into a marginally profitable one, even after splitting the plunder with the Huguenots. Drake hoped to return to pick up the buried silver, but a French straggler had been captured by the Spanish, then tortured until he revealed where the treasure had been buried. When Drake learned of this fresh disaster he decided to return home, and on 9 August the *Pasco* sailed into Plymouth, with just enough in its holds to warrant the 15-month-long raid.

The English share of the haul has been estimated at around 50,000 pesos, and even after dividing it amongst the crew and paying off investors, Drake still had a enough profit to clear his debts and to set himself up as a gentleman of modest standing. He also found himself something of a national celebrity. For the next two years Drake was busy elsewhere, campaigning in Ireland on behalf of the Queen, establishing a home with his new wife, and being presented at court. However, he also used this time to plan a new expedition, one even more ambitious than the last.

Drake's voyage into the Pacific

Although Drake spent two years doing other things, he also met influential courtiers, scientists and explorers, gathering what information he could about the South Sea, the region we now know as the Pacific Ocean. A plan evolved, whereby Drake would lead a small expedition into these largely uncharted waters and prey on Spanish shipping. At the same time he would gather whatever scientific and geographical information he could. In effect it would be a voyage of discovery, financed by plunder.

During the later 16th century, the Spanish regarded the Pacific as their own private ocean, and Spanish ships there were less well armed than those in the Caribbean. Spanish vessels transported silver northwards from Peru to Panama, and gold, spices and jewels from the Orient to Mexico. This last route, plied by the Manila galleons, was what interested Drake the most.

They represented the ultimate piratical prize, a source of fabulous wealth for anyone bold enough to venture halfway round the world to fight for the treasure.

Queen Elizabeth shared Drake's enthusiasm for the venture, and as plans took shape she became a secret shareholder in the expedition. For diplomatic reasons the English monarch was unable to be linked officially with the enterprise, but her sanction of it was widely known, and Drake's financial backers included her leading advisors: the Earl of Leicester, Sir Francis Walsingham, Christopher Hatton and Sir William Wynter. In effect, the voyage would be an unofficial state-sponsored pirate cruise. Drake was even sent detailed instructions, ordering him to pass through the Strait of Magellan, explore the Pacific coast of America and make contact with locals willing to trade with English merchants.

Drake sailed from Plymouth in November 1577, but was forced back into port by a storm. He set sail again on 13 December, flying his flag in the 120-ton *Pelican*. She was accompanied by four other ships: the 80-ton *Elizabeth* commanded by John Wynter, the 30-ton *Marigold* commanded by John Thomas, the 15-ton pinnace *Benedict* and the 50-ton supply ship *Swan*.

From the start, the voyage was marked by dissension. Off the coast of Morocco the *Benedict* was abandoned for a Portuguese prize called the *Christopher*. Another captured Portuguese trading ship was renamed the *Mary*, in honour of Drake's wife. He appointed Thomas Doughty to command her, but Drake soon suspected this new captain of plotting against him. He exchanged ships, placing Doughty in charge of the *Pelican*, presumably so that his activities could be watched more closely.

According to Drake, Doughty continued his seditious talk during the Atlantic crossing, and matters reached a head when the ships made landfall off the River Plate in mid March 1578. Drake transferred Doughty to the *Swan*, placing him under open arrest. From there the expedition sailed down the coast of South America, reaching Port St Julian near the entrance of the Magellan Strait on 18 June. It was there that Drake charged Doughty with inciting mutiny, and – bizarrely – of witchcraft. A trial was held, and as a result the unfortunate Doughty was sentenced to death, and then executed. The likelihood is that while Doughty was indeed a troublemaker, Drake decided he couldn't afford any questioning of his authority during the voyage that lay ahead. His draconian act quelled any further dissent. While in Port St Julian Drake abandoned the *Swan* after distributing its stores, burned the Portuguese prizes and re-named the *Pelican* the *Golden Hind*. All was ready for the next dangerous phase of the expedition – the voyage into the storm-tossed seas of the Magellan Strait.

On 20 August the *Golden Hind*, *Elizabeth* and *Marigold* put to sea, and a week later they entered the treacherous waters of the Strait, which lay between the island of Tierra del Fuego and the South American mainland. This dangerous transit took the best part of two weeks. All seemed to be going well until they neared the Pacific Ocean. Then they were hit by a violent storm, a tempest more severe than anything any of these veteran English seamen had ever experienced. The *Marigold* foundered with all

TABLA GEOGRAPHICA DEL REYNO DE CHILE

In this late 16th-century chart showing the southern tip of South America, east is at the top. The Magellan Strait, traversed by Drake in late 1577, is on the right, between the mainland and the island of Tierra del Fuego.

hands, while John Wynter in the *Elizabeth* and Francis Drake in the *Golden Hind* were separated by the storm, and the two captains would never see each other again until Drake's return to Plymouth two years later. After waiting for Drake off the Peruvian coast, Wynter decided to complete the voyage on his own. He thought about heading westward across the Pacific to the East Indies, a region Drake had expressed an interest in exploring. Instead he decided to return home the way he had come, and he arrived back in Plymouth in June 1579.

Drake was now left on his own. The storm had driven him far to the south, beyond the tip of Cape Horn and towards the icy perils of the Antarctic. When the tempest abated, he worked his way back to the north, hoping to encounter the *Elizabeth* somewhere off the South American coast. He continued northwards as far as the island of Mocha off the coast of Chile, which he reached on 25 November. This point marked the southern limit of

Spanish settlement. He continued on to the small port of Valparaiso, where on 5 December he captured and ransacked a Spanish merchant ship, and pillaged the town. This yielded plunder worth 25,000 pesos, and marked the start of Drake's piratical cruise.

At this point, Drake paused in a deserted anchorage to repair his battered ship and to take on water. He also built a small pinnace, which he towed astern. She would prove useful in the cutting-out raids that lay ahead. Drake then continued his cruise, and in early February 1579 he appeared off Arica, the port where silver from Potosi was loaded onto ships bound for Panama. There and in the neighbouring small ports he captured a handful of prizes yielding a small quantity of plunder, but nothing of any real value. It seems that the Spanish had warning of his coming, and landed a cargo of silver before he arrived. More importantly though, he captured and interrogated Spanish seamen, who told him that a treasure galleon was on its way to Panama, but was several days ahead of the *Golden Hind*. This was exactly the sort of rich prize Drake had been looking for. Drake decided to sail north and intercept her.

On the way he looked into Callao, the port serving Lima, the capital of the Viceroyalty of Peru. Once again he found little of any value, and he sped on to the north. However, what Drake did discover from Spanish fisherman was that the treasure galleon – the 120-ton *Nuestra Señora del la Concepción* – was only a few days ahead of him, and Drake's ship was faster. Drake had also learned that for some reason the Spanish nicknamed the galleon the '*Cacafuego*' (lit. 'shit-fire'), and that she was relatively lightly armed. All he had to do was to catch her.

Late in the day of 1 March 1579 a lookout – Drake's cousin John – sighted the galleon ahead of them. Rather than cram on sail, Drake had disguised his ship as a Spanish merchantman, and he streamed a kedge anchor astern to slow his ship down. This meant that while he gradually overhauled the Spanish galleon, the suspicions of her crew weren't aroused. When Drake finally made his move the Spanish were too close to escape. As a result, the Spanish captain San Juan de Anton, was taken completely by surprise.

As he approached the *Concepción*, Drake hauled down his Spanish colours and hoisted the St George Cross. He called upon the Spaniards to surrender, and when they refused he ordered his men to open fire. The mizzen mast of the Spanish galleon was brought down by the first broadside and within minutes Drake had sent his pinnace across with a boarding party. The Spaniards had no real option but to surrender. What the Englishmen discovered was a wealth of plunder. The hold of the *Concepción* contained chests filled with silver pesos, some 26 tons of silver ingots and 80lb of gold bars. That was just the official cargo. The total haul was later valued at 400,000 pesos – or £260,000 in English gold – roughly the equivalent of $75 million today. While this represented a mere 3 per cent of the annual total of specie that flooded into the Spanish coffers, it was an unbelievable windfall to Drake and his men, the richest prize of their lives.

All Drake had to do now was to sail home with his plunder, Unfortunately, the Spanish were now well aware where he was, and would be looking for him. The voyage back down the South American coast would take the English through waters that would be patrolled by Spanish warships eager for revenge. Drake decided to avoid the danger by taking the long way home – heading westwards across the Pacific, through the East Indies into the Indian Ocean, then sailing round Africa into the Atlantic, before heading northwards towards home. Drake's voyage would therefore be a complete circumnavigation of the globe.

Dramatic though this voyage was, the details of it lie beyond the scope of this book. In brief, he continued on to the north, keeping clear of the big Spanish ports of Panama and Acapulco. He sailed up the Pacific coast of North America as far as what is now Canada, possibly in the hope of discovering the western end of the fabled North-West Passage. All he found was ice. He retraced his route southwards to the level of what is now California. Drake spent several weeks there, in a region he dubbed 'Nova

During his voyage of raid into the Pacific Ocean in 1577 80, Francis Drake in his little ship *Golden Hind* attacked and captured the poorly armed Spanish treasure galleon *Nuestra Señora del la Concepción*, which was laden with silver and other specie.

Albion', possibly in the region of what has become San Francisco Bay. It was from there on 23 July 1579 that he headed west across the Pacific. Two months later he made landfall at an island he called the Island of Thieves, before continuing on towards the Philippines. He skirted them and headed south towards the Spice Islands of the East Indies.

After a brief sojourn at Ternate, Drake sailed for England, with six tons of cloves in his hold. Three of these had to be jettisoned when the ship ran aground somewhere off Timor, and it took two months to repair the ship and then cautiously sail her through the maze of islands into the deep blue waters of the Indian Ocean. By late March 1580, the *Golden Hind* had left Java astern, and ten weeks later she rounded the Cape of Good Hope. On 26 September Drake finally entered Plymouth Sound, after a voyage lasting just over 33 months.

Drake's first question when coming within hailing distance of a Devon fisherman was whether the Queen was in good health. Whatever her condition, she would have welcomed the news of Drake's return. After all, the Sea Dog had brought her a substantial return on her secretive investment. Drake found himself feted as a hero, and one of the wealthiest men in Devon. He also found that the country was on the brink of war, a conflict he had done much to bring about.

In April 1581, the Queen honoured Drake by visiting his ship as it lay at anchor in Deptford on the River Thames. She celebrated the event by knighting him on the quarterdeck of the *Golden Hind*, which had been repainted and draped with bunting for the occasion. This event was a very visible sign that the political climate had changed. By formally acknowledging the man Queen Elizabeth called 'my pirate' she was sending a clear signal to the Spanish that English attitudes towards them were hardening. For years Drake and his compatriots had walked a diplomatic tightrope as England and Spain were embroiled in a 'Cold War'. Now it seemed that the diplomatic gloves were about to come off. This meant that Sir Francis Drake's private war with the Spanish was about to become part of a larger international struggle.

PLANNING THE RAID

The background

Relations between England and Spain had been deteriorating steadily for a quarter of a century, ever since the accession of Queen Elizabeth in late 1558. By 1584 they had reached an all-time low. Religion lay at the heart of the problem. Elizabeth was a Protestant, as were the majority of her subjects, while King Philip II of Spain was a devout Catholic, and a staunch supporter of the Counter-Reformation. The imprisonment of the Catholic Mary, Queen of Scots in 1568 and the Hawkins expedition which ended in the same year did little to improve diplomatic relations, nor did Elizabeth's covert support for the Dutch Protestants, who revolted against Spanish rule during the early 1570s. These events were followed by Drake's two expeditions of 1572–74 and 1577–80. Elizabeth's open admiration for a man the Spanish viewed as a pirate only served to heighten the tension.

Drake's raid into the Pacific coincided with a major Spanish offensive in the Netherlands. From 1578 to 1580 the Duke of Parma's Spanish veterans succeeded in driving the rebels from what is now Belgium, until only Antwerp remained in Protestant hands. It was then only a matter of time before Parma captured the city. Then in 1580 the Spanish invaded Portugal, and captured their neighbouring country after a lightning campaign. The spoils included a powerful squadron of Portuguese galleons, and two years later these warships were at the forefront of a naval campaign that saw the Spanish fleet emerge victorious over the remnants of the Portuguese and their French allies. Spain now had naval muscle, and seemed willing to use it.

The Spanish were also intervening closer to home. In late 1580 a small Spanish expedition was sent to Ireland, to encourage a general Catholic rising there. The English fleet blockaded the Spanish at Smerwick on Ireland's west coast, and the expeditionary force was eventually compelled to surrender. In 1584 the English began planning an expedition designed to establish a colony in the Americas, a land the Spanish regarded as their own. Also in 1584 the Spanish negotiated a treaty with the French Catholics, providing men, money and arms to help drive the Huguenots from French soil. Each of these

Here is another depiction of an Elizabethan warship, this time showing the *White Bear* (732 tons), one of the most powerful vessels in the royal fleet. Both this engraving and the complementary one of the *Golden Lion* on p.14 were drawn by Claes Jansz Visscher.

incidents served to increase the political tension, and showed that Philip II was embarked on a crusade on behalf of the Catholic Church.

While war wasn't inevitable in 1584, it was probably the last chance for peace. Elizabeth and her advisors honestly believed that by launching an expedition against the Spanish they would be able to deter Philip from going on the offensive against them. That would buy time for the diplomats to avert a conflict. Since his return to England in 1580 Drake had been arguing that a strike of this kind was needed, especially if the English could find a way of exploiting Portuguese and Spanish rivalry. Drake originally proposed an expedition to the East Indies, and as late as November 1584 the merits of this plan were being debated by Elizabeth's counsellors, including the Earl of Leicester and John Hawkins. In the end, political developments led to a change of plan.

In early 1585, Queen Elizabeth ordered negotiations to be opened with the Dutch, whereby England would recognize their independence and become their ally and protector. In May, Philip responded by ordering the seizure of all English shipping in Spanish ports. Both sides were increasing the stakes in a game of brinkmanship. Elizabeth's response was to use Drake to raise the stakes even further. He would be invited to visit the ports of Spain, and demand the return of the ships, or recompense. If it wasn't forthcoming, then pre-arranged letters of reprisal would come into effect, and he would therefore be able to attack the Spanish and plunder their own ships and towns, by way of reprisal. This then was the political foundation of the expedition. However, like any Elizabethan venture of this kind, it would be organized as a financial as well as a military or naval venture.

Organization

Drake's expedition was organized as a joint-stock enterprise. That meant that various individuals put up a stake in the venture, in money, ships, men or resources. They all expected a return in the form of a share of the plunder. No plunder meant no profit for the investors. The names of the principal shareholders remain a secret, but almost certainly they included Queen Elizabeth, the Earls of Bedford, Leicester, Rutland and Shrewsbury, John and William Hawkins, Walter Raleigh, Sir Christopher Hatton and Sir Francis Drake himself.

Most of these men contributed ships to the expedition. The Earl of Leicester provided the tiny *Speedwell* and the purpose-built 400-ton privateer *Galleon*

THE *ELIZABETH BONAVENTURE*, 1585–86

During his great raid on the Spanish Main (1585–86) Sir Francis Drake used the royal warship *Elizabeth Bonaventure* as his flagship. She was a fairly elderly vessel, having been bought by the Royal Exchequer from an English shipowner in 1567. The vessel herself was of course even older than that, and it has been suggested she was first built during the reign of Queen Mary (1553–58). At the time she was described as a 'galleon', of around 600 tons.

In 1581 she was extensively rebuilt by Sir John Hawkins, and she emerged from the royal shipyard in Deptford as a new vessel – a 'race-built galleon', a faster and more manoeuvrable English version of the Spanish galleon. Part of this rebuilding involved reducing her superstructure, and turning her into a sleek four-masted warship of 448 tons.

The *Elizabeth Bonaventure* was less than 100ft long at the waterline, and just 120ft overall, with a beam of 52ft. These dimensions made her a good gun platform, and she mounted an imposing armament for a ship of her size – 39 guns, including two demi-cannon, 11 culverins and 14 demi-culverins. She performed well during the expedition, and so Drake retained her as his flagship during his raid on Cadiz in 1587, and his pursuit of the Spanish treasure fleets later that same year. She outlived both Francis Drake and Queen Elizabeth, and was finally sent to the breaker's yard in 1611.

Drake's land commander, Lieutenant-General Christopher Carleill was an experienced soldier, having fought in the Spanish Netherlands before joining forces with Drake. He proved to be an inspiring leader, and led his soldiers to victory at Santo Domingo and Cartagena.

Leicester, commanded by his brother-in-law Francis Knollys. Sir William Wynter provided the *Sea Dragon*, Lord Howard of Effingham supplied the *White Lion* (commanded by Captain Erisey), while the Hawkins brothers offered the *Bark Bond* (Robert Crosse), the *Bark Bonner* (George Fortescue), the *Bark Hawkins* (William Hawkins), the *Hope* and the *Galliot Duck* (Richard Hawkins). Drake's own ships included the *Thomas Drake* (commanded by its namesake), the *Elizabeth Drake* (John Vamey) and the *Francis* (Thomas Moone), but he flew his flag in a royal warship, the *Elizabeth Bonaventure*.

The Queen's stake was £10,000 in money and two ships – the 600-ton *Elizabeth Bonaventure* and the 250-ton *Aid*. Their joint value was placed at £10,000, a deliberate over-valuing to enable the monarch to draw a larger profit from the expedition than she would otherwise be entitled to. In fact, she wasn't the stakeholder here – it was the English taxpayer, operating in her name. Her only tangible benefit from a successful expedition would have been the political discomfiture of her rival monarch. Both ships had been rebuilt, and Drake's flagship was regarded as being a particularly impressive vessel. Other ships were supplied by London merchants, or their counterparts from West Country ports.

This expedition was therefore not purely a great piratical or privateering raid – it was a commercial enterprise, with carefully laid down goals. By diverting New World revenue from Spanish to English coffers, Elizabeth and her fellow backers were depriving the Spanish of the resources they needed to wage war, while increasing their own ability to defend themselves and their Dutch allies. In Elizabethan England business, politics and privateering were all hopelessly intertwined. As admiral, Drake commanded a force of 29 ships of various sizes, from the *Elizabeth Bonaventure* down to small 20-ton pinnaces. His deputy – or vice-admiral – was Martin Frobisher, a highly experienced but harsh seaman from Yorkshire who had already made his name as both a privateer and an Arctic explorer. He flew his flag in the

In this detail of the engraving by Theodore de Bry, the English fleet is depicted lying at anchor off Santo Domingo. The *Elizabeth Bonaventure* was the largest vessel in the fleet, and is identifiable as Drake's flagship, as it is shown flying the royal standard.

400-ton *Primrose*, supplied by London merchants. The Lieutenant-General of the expedition, Christopher Carleill, who commanded all land forces, hoisted his standard in another London ship, the 150-ton *Tiger*. Carleill was a stepson of Sir Francis Walsingham, and an experienced soldier and would-be explorer. Together these men commanded the largest fleet England had ever sent into American waters.

Carleill's force consisted of 12 companies of soldiers – around 1,600 men – and while these troops were largely inexperienced, Carleill himself knew his business, as did his sergeant-major (the equivalent of a major-general) Anthony Powell, and his two 'Corporals in the Field' (the equivalent of colonels), Matthew Morgan and John Simpson. Together these officers would make sure that the soldiers did what was expected of them. If we add the seamen to the total, Drake commanded almost 2,300 men and boys. He managed to avoid being encumbered with too many courtiers and adventurers. These included Sir Fulke Greville, Sir Philip Sidney and the adventurer Don Antonio, all of whom were left behind when Drake sailed. This meant that for the most part Drake's officers and men were seasoned professionals, and it was unlikely that he would encounter the same dissent that had hindered him during his voyage to the Pacific.

Although he was a renowned explorer, privateer and Elizabethan 'Sea Dog' in his own right, Martin Frobisher (c. 1539–94), Drake's naval second-in-command, was content to let his admiral make the decisions, and merely provided him with experienced counsel.

The objective

Drake already had his official instructions, and he had been fully briefed on the need to go through the motions of demanding redress from the Spanish. He also realized that this was little more than a diplomatic nicety. His real objective was the Spanish Main, where it was expected that he would raid the Spanish colonies, disrupt their trade and ideally intercept the annual treasure *flota*. For once he had the ships and men he needed to tackle this powerful Spanish force head-on. Sir Francis Walsingham – Elizabeth's foreign policy advisor and 'spymaster' – told Drake that he hoped the hardest possible blow would be struck by him.

This voyage was therefore seen by Walsingham as a pre-emptive rather than a diplomatic measure, aimed at depriving the Spanish King of the wherewithal to wage a naval war against England. It was up to Drake how he would carry this out. After all, he knew the Caribbean like few other Englishmen, and he had spent years studying Spanish strengths and weaknesses in the New World. Drake was one of the few men who could fulfil these political objectives while satisfying the expedition's shareholders at the same time. This said, as September drew to a close Drake was eager to sail. His dread would be a last-minute recall, as the Queen had second thoughts about launching this risky strike against the Spanish New World. In the end, Drake would sooner sail before all his preparations were ready than miss the chance to continue his own private war against the Spanish, this time with the resources he needed to inflict a telling blow against his enemies.

THE GREAT EXPEDITION

The island of Hispaniola, from a Spanish chart dated 1568, the year Drake and Hawkins were attacked at San Juan de Ulúa. In this depiction of the island three ships are shown sailing towards Santo Domingo, on the island's southern coast.

Drake's expedition set sail from Plymouth on 14 September 1585. The departure was so hurried that supplies were left on the quayside, and the ships lacked a full supply of water. Stores had been loaded onto the nearest ships rather than the ones they had been earmarked for, and the mess would take time to sort out – yet Drake wasn't prepared to do so in Plymouth. Once out to sea the die was cast, and there was no possibility of a last-minute postponement or cancellation from the Queen. Drake's haste is typified by the contract of Captain John Martin, which was hurriedly signed by Drake that very morning amid a rushed bid to sort out all the legal paperwork. It seemed that Drake realized that his raid was a politically sensitive enterprise, and it would take very little to persuade the Queen and his advisors that the whole project was a diplomatic time-bomb.

The expedition was the largest force Drake had ever commanded, and while he might have been nervous, this didn't show when he gathered together his principal commanders and captains on board the *Bonaventure* late that afternoon, as the fleet lay off the Cornish coast. He gave these officers his final sailing instructions, something that should have been done on shore, before the expedition sailed. He also laid down the law, issuing rules for the good governance of the expedition. This time there would be no repeat of the disharmony of his Pacific voyage.

Christopher Carleill recorded his impression of Drake at the gathering: 'For my own part I cannot say that ever I had to deal with a man of greater reason or more careful circumspection.' It seemed that the fiery Drake was learning the value of diplomacy.

Vigo

Drake's main concern was his supplies. As we have seen, the rush to leave Plymouth meant that stores were unevenly distributed throughout the fleet, and some vessels were already borrowing casks of food and water from their consorts. Drake refused to put into an English port to sort out the issue, as he still feared a recall from the Queen. The ships were crowded – the formula of one man for every 1½ tons of ship displacement was high, even by the standards of the time. Drake knew that they needed more supplies. He proposed a landing

The route taken by Drake on his 'Great Expedition'.

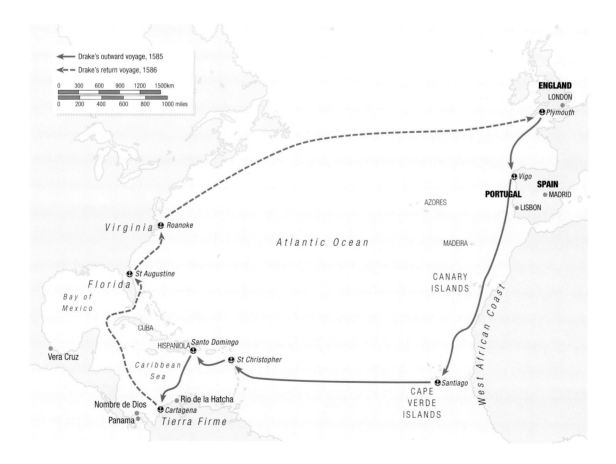

in either Ireland or France, but the latter was preferable, as it involved no risk of running into a royal messenger.

Drake's supply problem was sorted out more through luck than anything else. On 22 September, a large Spanish fishing boat was spotted, and the *Elizabeth Bonaventure* and *Tiger* set off in pursuit. It was Carleill in the *Tiger* who overhauled her first, and found that the holds of the Biscayan ship were laden with fish. After these were distributed throughout the fleet, Drake had enough supplies to last until he reached the Spanish coast. Once there he could seize whatever provisions he needed.

Five days later the fleet reached Vigo Bay, in the north-west corner of Spain, and it dropped anchor in the mouth of the River Vigo. The arrival presented Governor Don Pedro Bermudez in nearby Bayona with a problem. One of the most feared enemies of Spain was anchored off the port, and it was poorly defended. Although England and Spain were theoretically at peace, Drake's appearance suggested he didn't have peaceful intentions. Without instructions from Madrid, though, Don Pedro was unwilling to open fire. Drake solved the dilemma by offering to negotiate. He sent a messenger ashore, who asked two questions. First, was Spain at war with England? Second, why had the Spanish impounded English ships?

While he waited for his answer, Drake inspected the defences of Vigo and Bayona, and landing parties were sent to nearby islands to take on water. While there they desecrated a Catholic chapel, but Don Pedro was eager not to make an issue of this act. Instead his response was diplomatic. He told Drake that the two countries were at peace, and announced that although English shipping had been seized on orders of the King, the vessels had now been released. The message was accompanied by boat-loads of supplies – bread, oil and wine – a gift from the people of Galicia. He was obviously trying to placate the Englishmen. Drake responded by moving further up the river, so his guns threatened Vigo itself. Actually, this move was forced on the fleet by the weather; a storm was brewing, and they needed to move from their exposed anchorage in the mouth of the river. Don Pedro responded by gathering his militia on the city waterfront – 1,000 men, including cavalry.

With a major diplomatic incident brewing, Drake offered to talk again. He sent two captains ashore as hostages, and in return the Spanish governor was rowed out to meet Drake. The English commander in turn was rowed out to meet him, and in one of the most curious negotiating scenes of all time they talked for two hours, and managed to diffuse the explosive situation. Drake agreed to leave Vigo alone, if he could provision and water his ships without Spanish interference. The English fleet remained off the port for the best part of two weeks, and English sailors brazenly walked through the streets, protected by the firepower of Drake's ships. During this sojourn, Drake learned that he had missed his opportunity to intercept the returning Spanish treasure fleet. Part of it had returned safely to Seville before Drake had even set sail from England, while the rearguard was due to arrive any day. It seemed that the English were too late.

When Drake's fleet finally sailed from Vigo on 11 October, Don Pedro Bermudez must have been a relieved man, but he still had to answer for his actions to the King. After all, Drake had dictated terms on Spanish soil, and extorted supplies virtually at gunpoint. Attacks on Spain's colonies were one thing, but similar incidents in Spain itself were seen as a grave insult – an international humiliation. Worse, the Spanish had no idea where Drake would go next. King Philip ordered that the settlements in the New World be warned that Drake was at sea. The truth is, there was little he could do. While the defences of the Spanish Main were strong enough to resist small groups of interlopers, they were no match for Drake's fleet. All of Spain's key towns in the New World were now at risk, and there was no fleet on hand to protect them. It was little wonder that the Spanish viewed Drake as such a fearsome opponent. King Philip's empire lay at the mercy of a man who had little pity for the Spanish.

Santiago

Part of the reason Drake lingered so long in Vigo was the weather. A storm was raging, and there was little point putting to sea until it passed, and all the necessary provisions were loaded. Drake still hoped to intercept the rearguard of the Spanish treasure fleet. The English fleet sailed down the Portuguese coast, by which time the *flota* was just leaving the Azores, having taken on stores and provisions there. That put them 930 miles to the east of Drake. However, the Spanish made a fast passage, and Drake was still off Lisbon when they slipped past the southern tip of Portugal – Cape St Vincent – some 125 miles to the south. From there the *flota* reached the safety of the Guadalquivir River by the middle of the month. This meant that Drake missed this huge opportunity by less than a day.

In this engraving by Theodore de Bry depicting Drake's assault on the town of Santiago in the Cape Verde Islands, the Spanish townspeople are shown fleeing from the English troops advancing from the east, while Drake's fleet lies just outside the harbour.

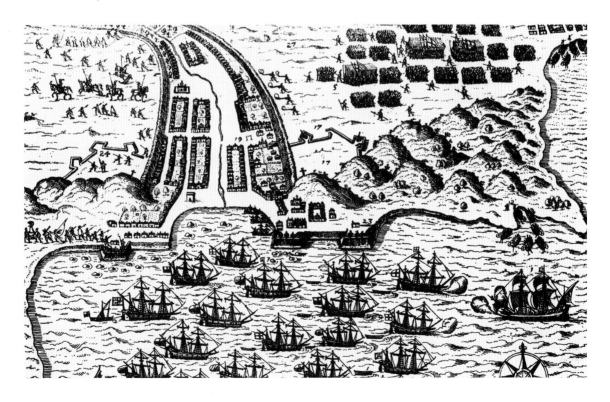

DRAKE'S ASSAULT ON SANTIAGO, CAPE VERDE ISLANDS

11 NOVEMBER 1585

Sir Francis Drake launched his first assault on a Spanish town before he had even crossed the Atlantic. In November 1585, he appeared off the small port of Santiago, the capital of the Cape Verde Islands, which until five years before had been in Portuguese rather than Spanish hands. In this attack Drake demonstrated the tactics that would serve him well in the Caribbean – a naval 'demonstration' off the port, while an assault force moved into position to launch a surprise attack from land.

KEY

A English fleet (Drake)

B The English assault force (Carleill) – 1,000 men in 18 companies

C The town's principal coastal batteries

D Secondary harbour battery

E Spanish earthworks (Fortalezza San Filipe)

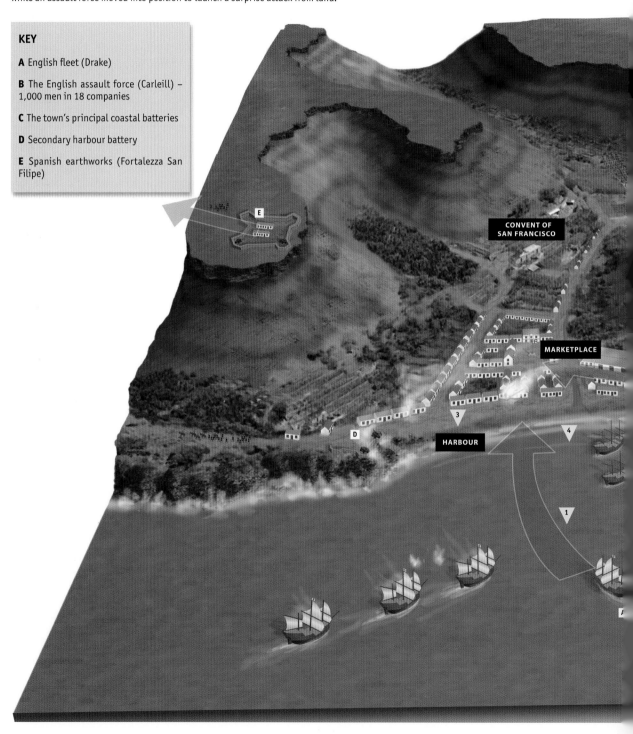

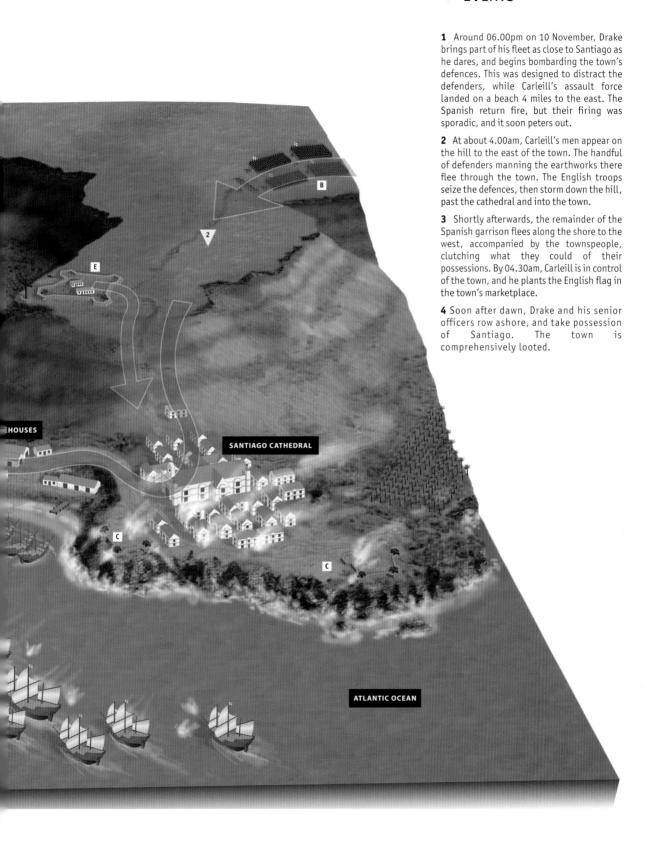

▼ EVENTS

1 Around 06.00pm on 10 November, Drake brings part of his fleet as close to Santiago as he dares, and begins bombarding the town's defences. This was designed to distract the defenders, while Carleill's assault force landed on a beach 4 miles to the east. The Spanish return fire, but their firing was sporadic, and it soon peters out.

2 At about 4.00am, Carleill's men appear on the hill to the east of the town. The handful of defenders manning the earthworks there flee through the town. The English troops seize the defences, then storm down the hill, past the cathedral and into the town.

3 Shortly afterwards, the remainder of the Spanish garrison flees along the shore to the west, accompanied by the townspeople, clutching what they could of their possessions. By 04.30am, Carleill is in control of the town, and he plants the English flag in the town's marketplace.

4 Soon after dawn, Drake and his senior officers row ashore, and take possession of Santiago. The town is comprehensively looted.

B

2

E

EHOUSES

SANTIAGO CATHEDRAL

C

C

ATLANTIC OCEAN

The disappointment must have been great. By intercepting all or part of the returning treasure *flota*, Drake would have struck the Spanish a crippling blow. He would also have earned himself and his country a staggering fortune. Instead he headed southwards to the Canary Islands, where he hoped to take on more provisions before he began his transatlantic voyage.

By 3 November the fleet was lying off Las Palmas, where Drake planned to land and seize whatever provisions and plunder he could find. Unfortunately for the English, the sea was too rough to attempt a landing, and the Spanish gunners plied the approaching English ships with shot. One roundshot narrowly missed Drake and his two leading officers as they stood on the quarterdeck of the *Elizabeth Bonaventure*. Other hits were scored against the *Galleon Leicester* and the *Aid*. Quite sensibly Drake decided to withdraw. Instead he took on water from the undefended island of Gomera, and then continued his voyage, heading south towards the Cape Verde Islands.

These islands were a strange destination. Drake's orders were explicit – to sail to the Caribbean, and to attack Spanish settlements there. There was no mention of the Cape Verde Islands, a relatively poor archipelago that until five years ago had been Portuguese, but was now controlled by Spain. Drake later argued that he intended to set off from there on his transatlantic voyage. After all, this was fairly common practice. However, a more direct course would have been to use the Canary Islands as a springboard for the Atlantic crossing. It has been argued that Drake needed provisions, as he had been thwarted in taking on stores at Las Palmas. It was also claimed to be a diversion, putting the Spanish off his trail before he descended on the Spanish Main.

A more likely reason is revenge. Three years before, William Hawkins – the father of John and William the Younger – had visited the Cape Verde Islands with seven ships, two of which belonged to Drake or his brothers. Although this was a peaceful trading voyage the Spanish garrison there had launched a surprise attack against the moored English ships, and the elder Hawkins lost several of his men before he could escape to safety. This episode was too much like the humiliation of San Juan de Ulúa for Drake to ignore. In his account of the voyage the Elizabethan chronicler Thomas Cates even claimed that Drake gave his reason for the punitive attack on Santiago in the Cape Verde Islands as being the 'fresh remembrance of the great wrong they had done to old Mr. William Hawkins of Plymouth, in the voyage he made four or five years before, when they did both break their promise, and murthered many of his men'. Here was little more than a continuation of Drake's private war.

The town of Santiago (Sào Tiago) lay on the south-west side of the island of the same name, the largest island in the Cape Verde archipelago. It is now called Cidade Velha ('Old City' in Portuguese), and at the time it served as a major base for Portuguese slaving operations on the West African coast, and was an exporter of both sugar and cloth. When Drake arrived in November 1585 it had a population of around 2,000 people, and its white-walled and red-roofed buildings were surrounded by lush groves of palm, fig and citrus trees. The town itself lay at the head of a narrow valley, flanked by barren and precipitous hills, and was protected by two batteries that covered the anchorage. These sat on a small headland in the centre of the town, while a third was sited on lower ground to the west, covering the landward approach to the town from the beach. While these defences sounded imposing, they had not been maintained, and offered little protection against Drake and his men.

On the evening of 11 November, Christopher Carleill landed his men in what was almost certainly their first amphibious landing. It would also be their first taste of a night march and night battle. More than 1,000 troops landed without any major mishap, and under cover of darkness Carleill led his men into position on the eastern side of the town, stumbling through the rock and brush as they went. This side of the town was unprotected – the defences were concentrated on its seaward side, covering the anchorage and the beach.

The Baptista Boazio map of 1588 makes Santiago look far more orderly than it really was. However, it shows the harbour was merely a small curved beach, with a small quayside on the western edge of the rocky promontory. It could hold nothing more than a few small fishing boats; anything larger had to anchor further out in the bay. The town sat astride the stream, while the small headland was dominated by a diminutive cathedral, with the stream on its western side. Boazio omitted the church, built in the late 15th century, but marked its location with a small chapel. He also got the hinterland wrong, as the town sat in a hollow surrounded by high, arid hills. In his version, Carleill is advancing towards the town across a level plain, presumably a simplified depiction of the plateau that all but surrounded the small port.

As Carleill moved into position Drake brought up his ships and began bombarding the shore batteries. They fired back, but their response was lacklustre, and soon Drake and his men could see the townspeople fleeing to safety, heading west, away from Carleill and his soldiers. In the end there was no resistance worth speaking of. After a few shots the batteries fell silent, and Carleill marched into an undefended, empty town. The only inhabitants who remained were a few elderly residents, and 26 fever-ridden patients in the slave hospital. By dawn the Cross of St George was flying over the town, and Drake landed to see what the locals had left behind them.

There was little to plunder. The English captured seven Portuguese slave ships lying at anchor off the town. One of them was added to the fleet, while the rest were stripped of anything of value. Drake's men looted what they could. Old bronze Portuguese guns and equipment were taken from the batteries, silk and cloth were seized from the town's warehouses, the houses were ransacked for food and the groves stripped of their fruit. Drake's men even took the bronze bell from the town's cathedral. Drake sent emissaries to track down some of the inhabitants, as he planned to hold the town and burn it unless the island's governor paid him a ransom. Nobody came forward to negotiate.

The few locals he captured told him that the governor was in the nearby village of Santo Domingo (São Domingos), a few miles inland. Drake and Carleill led a force of 600 men in a dispiriting trek into the arid hills of Santiago island. The inhabitants of Santo Domingo fled when the English

The landing of Lieutenant-General Carleill's men a few miles to the east of Santiago, from a detail of a one of a series of coloured engravings produced by Baptista Boazio in 1588, to celebrate Drake's accomplishments during the expedition of 1585–86.

approached, so Drake and his men looted what little they could, then burned the village to the ground. The punitive expedition returned to the coast, shadowed as they went by Spanish cavalry. The only fatality was a teenage English straggler, who was captured and executed by the vengeful Spaniards.

On 28 November, Drake made one last attempt to force the Spanish governor to pay a ransom. He sent Carleill on another expedition 9½ miles along the coast to the east, until he reached the small settlement of Porto Praia (now simply Praia, the capital of the island). Carleill's arrival coincided with the appearance of Drake and the fleet off the town's beach at dawn the following morning. Once again the 1,000 or so inhabitants fled to safety, leaving Drake in control of another empty town. Similarly, he ordered it to be razed to the ground, sparing only the town hospital, but there was no plunder worth having.

Drake's severity was his way of sending the Spanish a message. He wanted to make a handsome profit from his raids, and he was simply telling the Spanish that if they refused to negotiate a ransom with him the English would have no hesitation in destroying any town they captured. Drake probably hoped that word of these events would reach the Spanish Main ahead of him, so that other Spanish townspeople might be more willing to part with their wealth in order to spare their homes. In fact, Drake's standing orders were designed to protect Spanish property, in an attempt to encourage the payment of a ransom. If any plunder was found it would be kept safe, so it could be distributed equitably.

As Drake's orders put it:

> For as much as we are bound in conscience and required also in duty to yield an honest account of our doings and proceedings in this action … persons of credit shall be assigned, unto whom such portions of goods of special price, as gold, silver, jewels, or any other thing of moment or value, shall be brought and delivered, the which shall remain in chests under the charge of four or five keys, and they shall be committed into the custody of such captains as are of best account in the fleet.

Back in Santiago, Drake had another problem to deal with. Captain Francis Knollys of the *Galleon Leicester* was a nobleman who saw Drake as a parvenu. As an in-law of the Earl of Leicester he imagined himself as beyond the reproach of Drake, and for months he had spread discord, questioning Drake's actions and demanding a greater say in decision making. His diary shows how deeply he disliked both Drake and Carleill, and believed that the pair had deceived him by keeping plunder for themselves. In effect, he was accusing the two commanders of corruption, of robbing their fellow members of the expedition. The problem was brought out into the open on 20 November, when all captains were asked to swear loyalty to their sovereign, and to Drake as her appointed representative. Knollys refused to swear the oath, although he added that he would willingly declare his allegiance to the Queen. The following day – a Sunday – Drake's chaplain Philip Nichols decried Knollys in his sermon, claiming that anyone unwilling to swear the oath was unworthy of the expedition.

That evening Knollys confronted the cleric at Drake's dinner table, forcing the admiral to intervene. Drake railed at Knollys, accusing him of inciting sedition – even Drake balked at using the word 'mutiny'. Knollys replied that it would be best if Drake let him sail off on his own. The following morning, Drake was rowed over to the *Galleon Leicester*, and called its crew together. He asked them if they preferred to leave the expedition with Knollys, or remain with Drake. All but 40 or so elected to stay. Drake then declared that Knollys and his small band of followers were exempt from further service, and would be given the small *Francis* to sail home in. First, though, Drake had to protect himself. He demanded a written letter from Knollys, stating that he was prepared to leave Drake's expedition, and the service of the Queen, and return directly to England. Knollys agreed to two of the points, but refused to admit he was leaving the Queen's service. That would leave him open to later charges of desertion.

This wasn't good enough for Drake. He wanted rid of the aristocratic troublemaker, but he didn't want Knollys undermining Drake's position in the court. Instead he decided to keep Knollys with him on board the *Elizabeth Bonaventure* for the time being, where he could be watched. His men were distributed throughout the other ships of the fleet. Once again, Drake's actions appear draconian, but he was sensitive to insubordination, especially after the Thomas Doughty incident during his Pacific expedition. The whole oath of loyalty was unnecessary, and if it was administered anywhere it should have been done in Plymouth, before the expedition ever set sail. Drake left Santiago within a day of the capture of Porto Praia, but before he did so he ordered the town of Santiago to be razed – a final message to the Spanish. On the last day of November, his ships then headed westward, out into the Atlantic Ocean.

Santo Domingo

As far as we know, the garrison of the Cape Verde Islands only managed to inflict one casualty on the English – the teenage straggler. However, in reality they managed to inflict heavy losses on the expedition during the weeks that followed. Somehow the English had become infected by a virulent strain of fever, possibly contracted from the patients of the slave hospital. From what description we have of the symptoms it seems that it might have been a form of typhus, which spread through the crowded, unsanitary conditions on board the ships of the fleet. The crew of the *Elizabeth Bonaventure* suffered particularly badly – within days the majority of her crew were laid low with the fever. In just a fortnight almost a hundred of them were dead, while 60 more deaths were recorded on board the *Primrose*. The death tolls represented a third of each

Theodore de Bry's depiction of Drake's assault on Santo Domingo is clearly based on the earlier Boazio engraving, but they differ in minor details. The later version, for instance, accompanied an account of the battle, and was therefore annotated with a key.

ship's total complement. A strict quarantine was enforced, but nevertheless more than 300 English seamen and soldiers died before the fleet made its landfall in the West Indies. The survivors were left weak and debilitated, and in no condition to take part in an assault on a defended city.

Around 15 December, Drake arrived off Dominica in the Leeward Islands, where he took on water. He then moved north to the uninhabited St Christopher (St Kitts), where he landed his sick and fumigated his ships. He also probably took the opportunity to careen the vessels, cleansing their hulls of weeds and barnacles. No doubt he also acquired whatever fruit and game his men could find on the island. While all this was going on Drake sent a small scouting squadron off to the west, to conduct a reconnaissance of the Spanish-held island of Hispaniola. Drake intended to make the island's capital of Santo Domingo his next target.

Santo Domingo was once the capital of Spain's New World Empire, and it was a small, bustling city, perched on the south-eastern shore of Hispaniola in what is now the Dominican Republic. It was also the oldest Spanish city in the Americas. Known as the 'Flower of the West', its attractions included a substantial cathedral, monasteries, imposing civic buildings and shady tree-lined squares. Unlike Santiago in the Cape Verde Islands, this was a real city, worthy of attack. It was also an ecclesiastical, legal and administrative centre, the bureaucratic heart of the Spanish New World. Striking there would send a signal that no Spanish city in the Americas was safe from English attack.

The principal fortification in Santo Domingo was the Fortaleza Ozama, a strongpoint overlooking the harbour, and dominated by the stone keep of the Torre de Homenaje (Tower of Homage) – marked here as '26'. Unfortunately for the Spanish, the landward defences of the city were much less formidable.

DRAKE'S ASSAULT ON SANTO DOMINGO, HISPANIOLA

1 JANUARY 1586

At Santo Domingo, Drake perfected the tactics he developed in the Cape Verde Islands seven weeks earlier. He landed Major-General Carleill's assault force under cover of darkness, then as dawn rose he appeared off the town with his fleet. He bombarded the town and launched a dummy amphibious landing, and just when the Spanish were convinced the assault would come from the sea, Carleill and his men burst out of the jungle, and stormed the city.

KEY

A English fleet (Drake)

B The English assault force (Carleill) – 1,000 men in 18 companies

C The Fortaleza Ozama

D Spanish militia (de Ovalle) deployed in defence of the beach

▼ EVENTS

1 At dawn (around 4.30am) on New Year's Day Drake's fleet arrives off Santo Domingo, and lies just inside gun range of the city's shore batteries. The garrison already had word of Drake's impending attack, and three blockships had already been scuttled between the sand spit and the shore, blocking the entrance to the city's small harbour. The two sides bombard each other, but the Spanish lack reliable powder, and Drake isn't willing to press the attack. After all, this is only a diversion.

2 The Spanish spend the morning improving their defences on the beach, protecting themselves against an amphibious attack. Many of the defenders begin sneaking back into the city, or run away into the jungle.

3 At noon Drake realizes that Carleill and his men are in place, and so he stages an attempted assault on the beach, to pin the defenders in place. His boats never actually come within small-arms range of the shore.

4 While this diversion was underway, Carleill and his English soldiers appear out of the jungle to the west of the city, and advance into the open, with drums beating and flags flying. The Spanish governor sends forwards skirmish troops to block their path, and stampedes a heard of cattle in the hope of disrupting the English. Both the skirmishers and the cattle soon disappear into the jungle to the north, driven off by fire from the English arquebusiers.

5 At approximately 12.30pm, Carleill storms the Lenba gate and enters the city. A simultaneous assault by his deputy Sergeant-Major Powell also succeeds in capturing another gate, closer to the beach. The English are now inside the city.

6 By 3.00pm the only Spanish force left in the area is the garrison of the Fortreza Ozama, which holds out until nightfall. At that point the defenders escape to safety across the river, under cover of darkness.

7 By nightfall Drake and the bulk of his men have landed from their ships, and while his men pillage the city, Drake establishes his headquarters inside Santo Domingo Cathedral.

Santo Domingo was fortified on its landward side by a city wall built in the early 1500s, its line punctuated by small turrets and gun positions. The Fortaleza Ozama – a strongly stone-built castle – overlooked the entrance to its small harbour, and although it was first built in 1503 its defences had been improved and updated over the intervening decades. The most significant of these later additions was a substantial gun battery on the southern face of the fort built in 1571, overlooking the seaward approaches to the town. A striking feature of the castle was the Torre de Homenaje (Tower of Homage), a stone keep dominating the mouth of the harbour. A small sandbar also protected the entrance to the harbour, forcing ships to pass close under the guns of the fort before they could reach the anchorage. A secondary gun battery covered the north-east approaches to the town.

The governor, Cristóbal de Ovalle, declared it to be amongst the strongest forts in Christendom, and it was certainly well provided with artillery batteries, covering its landward and seaward approaches. Unfortunately for the Spanish, these defences were less imposing than they appeared. Many of the guns were mounted on carriages whose woodwork was rotten, rendering them useless. The fort's magazines were almost empty, and what little powder stored there was reputedly of such poor quality that the few guns capable of firing lacked the power to fire much further than the sandbar.

Another weakness was that the *Audencia* of Santo Domingo lacked a regular garrison. The only troops available to it were the city militia, a force of as many as 800 men, up to 100 of whom were mounted. Civic volunteers would flesh out their ranks in time of need. Cristóbal de Ovalle, who was also the president of the *Audencia* and the Captain-General of Hispaniola,

At Santo Domingo, Drake landed Carleill's men on the Bajos de Haina (Haina Beach), and was guided through the treacherous reefs and sandbars lying off the Haina River mouth by a renegade pilot. Detail of the De Bry engraving.

claimed that he had 1,500 men available to him, a mixture of militiamen and townspeople. A Spanish chronicler later described these defenders as 'a few residents with pikes and lances which they had inherited from their fathers or grandfathers, conquerors of the land, and a few harquebusiers, though without gunpowder, bullets or other ammunition'. They would be no match for Carleill and his English soldiers.

After a week at St Christopher, Drake set sail again, leaving 20 freshly dug graves behind him, the last of his fever victims. He must have encountered his reconnaissance squadron as he sailed westwards, who told him that Santo Domingo looked too formidable to assault from the sea, but that they had found a good landing beach at the mouth of the River Haina, about 10 miles further to the west. That opportunity dictated Drake's plan – after landing Carleill and his men on the Bajos de Haina (Haina Beach), Drake would distract the Spaniards by threatening an attack from seaward. Carleill would then storm the unsuspecting defenders from the west. Drake had another stroke of fortune. He captured a handful of prizes during his voyage from St Christopher, including a vessel sent from Spain warning de Ovalle that Drake might attack him. He therefore knew that the Spanish at Santo Domingo weren't expecting him. He also captured a Spanish pilot, who warned him that the mouth of the Haina was protected by reefs and pounding surf, but he offered to help Carleill put his men ashore safely, no doubt encouraged by the threat of what Drake might do to him if he refused to co-operate.

Better still, Drake learned a little more about the city's defences. Apparently the governor was more concerned at the prospect of a slave

In this detail of Theodore de Bry's engraving of the English assault on Santo Domingo, Christopher Carleill's soldiers are shown advancing on the town, with blocks of pikemen flanked and preceded by smaller bodies of arquebusiers.

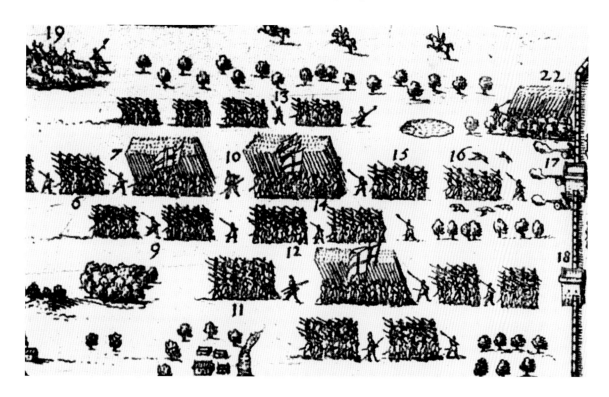

rebellion on the island, supported by the remnants of the local Carib Indians. Work had begun improving the crumbling western and northern defences of Santo Domingo, but a lack of funds and skilled labour meant that work had barely begun. Only a small section of the new defences had been completed around the western gate. The rest were barely high enough to prevent animals entering the city, let alone a determined band of armed men. The naval defences of the city consisted of one small patrol galley, and it was considered largely unseaworthy. Better still, the surf off the Bajos de Haina was considered so dangerous that they thought a landing there was impractical. Consequently the beach wasn't guarded, nor was the path through the jungle that led from it towards the city.

In this unusual coloured depiction of Santo Domingo and its environs, east is at the top of the map, where the landing place used by Drake at the mouth of the Haina River can be seen, with a track leading from it towards the town.

TO S DOMINGO.

Just after midnight on 1 January 1586 Drake arrived off the Bajos de Haina, and Carleill and his soldiers were safely set ashore. Drake accompanied the pilot as he guided the pinnaces through the reefs and surf, before returning to his flagship. Then the fleet sailed the 10 miles along the coast to Santo Domingo, so that Drake could see the city's defences for himself. By that stage a local fishing boat had already brought Cristóbal de Ovalle the news that a fleet was approaching, but by then it was too late. Troops were mustered, and three ships were sunk across the mouth of the harbour, to prevent any attempt to force the entrance. The small galley was stationed behind the sandbar, ready to fire on any English ship that tried to clear away the wreckage. Work began on building earthworks to defend the shore, and guns were wheeled into place to reinforce the seaward defences. It was all too little, and much too late. As labourers worked on the defences, many of the townspeople began slipping out of the city.

As dawn rose on New Year's Day, Drake's ships lay off the mouth of the harbour, just within artillery range. That was when Drake realized that the enemy's powder wasn't up to the task. One roundshot hit the *Elizabeth Bonaventure*, but most of the balls fell short. Drake ordered his ships in closer, and soon they began firing at the castle and the unfortunate militiamen in the rudimentary earthworks. With the Spanish distracted, Carleill and 800 soldiers approached the city, and by noon they were in position. As Drake made a show of attempting a landing by way of a diversion, Carleill and his men swept out of the jungle, appearing on the right flank of the Spanish militia with flags flying and drums beating. Cristóbal de Ovalle sent forward a skirmish line of cavalrymen and arquebusiers to protect his flank, but these were quickly driven back by

In this detail of a chart of Hispaniola drawn up in the early 17th century, the landward defences of Santo Domingo are no longer shown, while the Fortaleza Ozama (marked 'A' on the chart) protects the harbour from attack.

English fire. Next he tried herding cattle towards the English formations, but the animals simply ran off into the jungle. Within half an hour, the landing party had reached the western walls of Santo Domingo, and the majority of the city's militia were in flight.

The western defences were pierced by two gates: the Lenba (the main gate) and a secondary one, closer to the beach. By that stage there were scarcely 300 Spaniards left under arms, and most of them were woefully equipped with pikes and swords rather than firearms. Carleill ordered Sergeant-Major Powell to assault the secondary gate with a storming party, while the lieutenant-general led the rest of his men towards the Lenba. The defenders melted away, and neither column met with any serious opposition. The English were now inside the town. They began hunting the Spanish troops through the streets, heading towards the Fortaleza Ozama. While a small group of Spanish troops held out behind its walls, the remainder of the city was captured without any opposition. During the assault Carleill only suffered four casualties, and given the lack of serious resistance the Spanish losses were probably equally light.

Cristóbal de Ovalle had missed most of the battle, having fled the field soon after Carleill's men appeared on his flank. He later claimed that his horse had fallen in the muddy streets, and he had returned to his home to change his clothes before returning to the fray. The truth is he fled the city so precipitately that he left his wife behind, who became Drake's principal hostage. The fortress held out until nightfall, but under cover of darkness the remaining garrison slipped away by boat, and by dawn the English flag was flying over the Torre de Homenaje.

Drake ordered his men to repair the city's defences, in case of a Spanish counter-attack. Meanwhile their shipmates went on a looting spree, taking what they could from private homes, rifling through the civic offices and stealing the ornaments from the churches. The churches were singled out for special treatment: statues and windows were smashed, religious tapestries ripped down and altars desecrated. If Philip II wanted a religious crusade, Drake and his men would give it to him. The cathedral was spared the worst of these excesses only because that was where Drake set up his headquarters.

The plunder was disappointing. While plenty of goods were captured, including food and wine, only 16,000 gold ducats were recovered from the *Audencia*'s treasury – the equivalent of 32,000 pesos. Fortunately, Drake knew that this time the Spanish would be more willing to negotiate a ransom, in return for the saving of their town and the lives of his prisoners. On 12 January the head of the city judiciary, Juan Malarejo, approached Drake as the representative of Governor de Ovalle and the *Audencia*. Drake began the negotiations with a ludicrously high demand of a million ducats. Malarejo pleaded civic poverty, and as talks continued Drake ordered civic buildings and churches to be put to the torch, one after the other. The aim was to apply extra pressure on the unfortunate Malarejo, who returned to consult with his fellow officials. During the days that followed his men began demolishing the city's imposing stone buildings, even though they lacked the tools to make much of an impression.

The next Spanish negotiator was Garcia Fernandez de Torrequemada, the royal factor on Hispaniola. He proved even more stubborn than Malarejo, and after a week the best Drake could secure was a ransom of 25,000 ducats – or 50,000 pesos. It was far less than Drake had hoped, but he needed to continue his campaign of destruction. The deal was agreed, and Drake promised to spare what remained of the town and sail away from it if the ransom was paid promptly. In his report to the King, Torrequemada included his assessment of Drake:

> Francis Drake knows no language but English, and I talked with him through interpreters in Latin or French or Italian. He had with him an Englishman who understood a little Spanish, and who sometimes acted as interpreter. Drake is a man of medium stature, fair-haired, heavy rather than slender and jovial yet careful. He commands and rules imperiously, and is feared and obeyed by his men. He punishes resolutely. He is sharp, restless, well-spoken, inclined to liberality and to ambition, vain, boastful, and not notably cruel. These are the qualities I saw in him during my negotiations.

The comment about resolute punishment was soon put to the test. During these negotiations, Drake sent a delegation to the Spanish camp with a message. The party included a black boy who had joined Drake's force after the capture of the city. Although they approached the Spanish under a flag of truce, the boy was stabbed and killed by one of the Spaniards, possibly because he was recognized as a runaway slave. The dying boy was taken back to the city, and died in the cathedral, in front of Drake. The English commander was furious – it was said that nothing he did before or since ever matched his fury that day. He responded by having a gallows built within sight of the Spanish. He then had two prisoners brought out – Dominican monks – and they were hanged in full view of their horrified countrymen. A third prisoner was sent to the Spaniards, explaining why Drake had hanged the two clerics, and demanding they execute the murderer of the boy. Two more prisoners would be executed every day until the culprit was punished. The Spanish had little choice but to comply, and the murderer was duly executed within sight of the city.

Meanwhile, Drake solved the problem of Francis Knollys. The two men met on 10 January, and Drake offered Knollys a way out. If the captain swore the oath of loyalty, then Drake would pardon him, and name Knollys as his rear-admiral – second-in-command of the fleet after Vice-Admiral Martin Frobisher. Amazingly, Knollys refused the offer, and demanded to be sent home in the *Bark Hawkins*. Drake therefore rescinded the offer, and Knollys remained under house arrest until after the attack on Cartagena, by which time the expedition was returning home anyway. Fortunately, Drake's success at Santo Domingo meant that Knollys no longer posed a threat to the admiral's authority, and so he was able to ignore the peevishness of his subordinate.

The ransom was finally paid during the last days of January, and on 1 February the English sailed away from Santo Domingo, having occupied the city for exactly a month. A third of the city lay in ruins and almost all of its civic, military and religious buildings had been either damaged or

In this depiction of the assault on Santo Domingo, a detail from the engraving by Baptista Boazio, the artist has shown several stages of the action – the landing (bottom left), the approach march by Carleill and Drake's bombardment of the city's seaward defences.

destroyed. Upwards of 20 ships in the harbour were burned, and three vessels were commandeered by Drake to replace three small English ships that had to be abandoned as unseaworthy – the *Hope*, the *Benjamin* and the *Scout* (these were amongst the scuttled vessels). At least Cristóbal de Ovalle was reunited with his wife, although their home had been gutted. Garcia Fernandez de Torrequemada summed up the mood of the population in his report to the King: 'This thing must have had divine sanction, as punishment for the people's sins.' Drake certainly thought he had God on his side, albeit a Protestant rather than a Catholic one. It would take decades for the city to recover from Drake's onslaught.

As Drake disappeared over the horizon, news of his attack spread from Santo Domingo to other cities on the Spanish Main, warning that the Englishman was likely to descend on them. The trouble was, in whatever city Drake chose as his next target, the English fleet would outrun the news, and arrive there first. Within a month news of the attack had reached the Spanish

King, who had difficulty working out exactly what had been happening. He was being bombarded by conflicting accounts – Drake had been repulsed from the Canary Islands, he had burned half of Santiago island, his expedition was ravaged by disease, he had freed the slaves of Hispaniola, and he had sacked the 'Jewel of the West'. Other less accurate rumours claimed he had sacked other cities, including Havana, Cartagena and Vera Cruz. Even Pope Sixtus V heard the rumours, and explained, 'God only knows what he may succeed in doing.' Drake had become the talk of Europe.

The small city of Cartagena on the Spanish Main, as depicted in a detail from an early 17th-century chart. After Drake attacked it in 1586, the original town (I) was rebuilt, and expanded onto the small island in the salt marsh (1).

Cartagena des Indies

In fact, Drake was heading south towards Cartagena des Indies, the largest city on the Spanish Main. His original intention was to attack all the ports along the Spanish Main in turn, but his losses through disease made a protracted campaign inadvisable. Many of his men were still recovering from their fever, and a lengthy stay in such unhealthy waters was considered too great a risk.

Cartagena was the key to the Spanish Main. It was a major treasure port where gold and emeralds were stored, ready for shipment to Spain in the Tierra Firme *flota*. While the city itself was smaller than Santo Domingo, it was better defended, and Drake predicted that since his last visit to the port a decade before its defences would have been strengthened. While he didn't expect to extract a great deal of plunder, the capture and sack of Cartagena would be a major humiliation for the Spanish, and it would demonstrate that nowhere was safe from Drake and his men.

The trouble was, the inhabitants of Cartagena already knew he was coming. The first word of the English threat came from Seville – a galleon had been sent with a warning after Drake left Vigo. Then, while Drake was in Santo Domingo, a fast boat had sailed to Cartagena from Puerto Plata on the northern side of Hispaniola, bearing news that the city had been plundered, and warning them that Cartagena might be next. Governor Don Pedro Fernandez de Busto decided to take no chances. Anything of value was transported inland, while the city itself was evacuated of all non-essential residents or soldiers. Don Pedro Fernandez called for reinforcements from elsewhere in Venezuela, and the militia of Cartagena was mustered, equipped and drilled. Weapons were gathered and checked, fortifications were repaired and strengthened, and scouting craft were sent out to patrol the coast, and to provide warning of any approaching fleet. The governor was wise to be so cautious. Drake was on his way.

The English fleet made landfall on the Tierra Firme coast near Rio de la Hatcha, 240 miles to the west, then sailed along the coast towards Cartagena. This meant that Don Pedro had ample warning of Drake's approach, and reinforcements were ordered to the city, ready to defend it against a sudden assault. Drake knew Cartagena fairly well, having raided its harbour a decade before. He knew that the coast was a treacherous one, as the prevailing north-easterly winds made it hard for a fleet to anchor off the city. Not only were anchors likely to drag, but in a storm the vessels would face the perils of a lee shore, and would therefore need to claw their way out to the safety of the open sea.

Drake knew he needed to force his way through into one of two narrow channels, to reach the safer waters of the Outer Harbour. These channels – Boca Grande to the north and Boca Chica to the south – lay at either end of an island, now called Tierrabomba. While neither channel was fortified last time Drake was there, he fully expected the Spanish to have done so by now. The Outer Harbour was a sheltered anchorage about 6 miles long and 2 miles wide. The city itself lay at its northern end, which meant that once they breached the defences of the Outer Harbour, Drake's ships could anchor out of range of the Spanish guns, and he could plan the assault at leisure.

Cartagena lay on the coast, but it was well protected from attack on its seaward side, and the water there was too treacherous to permit a safe amphibious landing. The geography of the area was unusual. The city lay at the base of a narrow S-shaped spit of sand called La Caleta, which divided the Outer Harbour from the Caribbean, and which ended at the Boca Grande Channel. Another smaller island formed a bottleneck at the northern end of the Outer Harbour, and beyond this narrow channel – the Boquerón Channel – lay a small Inner Harbour, the main anchorage. The Inner Harbour was barely a mile long and half a mile wide, and the city itself formed its northern shore. Between Cartagena and the Venezuelan mainland, a seawater-filled moat had been dug, crossed by the fortified San Francisco bridge. To the east the land was swampy, and the wonderfully named Hanged Man's Swamp separated the city from the jungle-clad hills of the mainland. A single path wound its way through the swamp towards the fortified bridge, making a landward assault extremely difficult.

Drake appeared off Cartagena during the afternoon of 9 February 1586. He sailed right past the city itself, watched by the Spanish militia deployed along the city walls, and on the beach beyond. Drake was delighted to discover that the Boca Grande passage was unfortified, so his ships passed through it in a long column, with the *Elizabeth Bonaventure* in the lead. The English ships dropped anchor at the northern end of the Outer Harbour, just beyond the range of the Spanish guns guarding the Boquerón Channel. This passage into the Inner Harbour was guarded by El Boquerón, a stone-built fort with eight guns on its eastern side, commanded by Captain Pedro Mexia Mirabel. A chain boom ran across the entrance, protected on the La Caleta side by earthworks, supported by two small but well-armed galleys, the *Santiago* and the *Ocasión*. That afternoon, Drake sent Frobisher forward to probe the defences using small boats and pinnaces, but the English were driven back by a heavy fire from El Boquerón. Drake would have to come up with another plan.

Drake still had the best part of 1,800 men available, almost half of whom were soldiers. The number of troops available to Don Pedro Fernandez de Busto is harder to ascertain. Some 300 men crewed the two galleys, under the direct command of Don Pedro Vique y Manrique, who also doubled as the governor's military advisor. He was assisted by his two subordinates, Captain Juan de Castaneda in the *Santiago* and Captain Martin Gonzales in the *Ocasión*. (The crew figures didn't include a similar number of galley slaves, who were chained to their oars.) The fort of El Boquerón was garrisoned by about 200 men, mainly militia gunners, supported by a handful of Spanish regulars who served as officers and instructors. Another force of up to 570 militia protected the city itself (100 of them being pikemen), supported by a troop of 54 mounted lancers under the command of Captain Francisco de Carvajal, and a unit of as many as 400 Indian allies, equipped with bows and poisoned arrows. Compared to the force available to Governor de Ovalle in Santo Domingo, this was a veritable army.

The big difference between the two sides was morale. Drake and his men were buoyed up by their easy victories at Santiago and Santo Domingo, and they expected to win. Even the experienced soldier Don Pedro Vique recounted that despite the governor's speeches and the fact that they were defending their homes, neither man could instil much fighting spirit into the militia. Another disadvantage was they had no idea where Drake would launch his assault. This meant that troops had to defend El Boquerón and the Inner Harbour, the long spit of La Caleta and the city itself. By contrast,

At Cartagena, the English stormed the city's defences in a dawn attack. Despite being supported by fire from two galleys, the defenders were quickly routed, and the Englishmen poured into the city. Detail of a coloured engraving by Baptista Boazio.

Drake and Carleill could mass their assault force for one decisive thrust towards the city.

The governor decided to concentrate the bulk of his forces on La Caleta, between the Inner Harbour and the sea. There he ordered a line of entrenchments to be built, to protect the city behind him. The approach to these entrenchments was up the sandy spit, and the final stretch before the Spanish lines would be swept by gunfire from the two galleys patrolling the waters of the Inner Harbour. That way the superior numbers of the English could be offset by Spanish firepower and fortifications. Behind the earthworks the city itself was virtually defenceless. Despite being in office since Drake's last visit to Cartagena a decade before, Don Pedro Fernandez had failed to improve the city defences. Many of the guns were incapable of being fired, and the city walls were in a bad state of repair. Worse, on the southern side, facing La Caleta, the walls were virtually non-existent. If the English captured the earthworks, the city was bound to fall. Drake knew about these entrenchments, but he still thought that his best chance of capturing the city was by advancing up La Caleta. Carleill agreed, and together they concocted their plan.

Late in the evening of 9 February, the troops clambered into a cluster of waiting boats, and they were rowed across the Boca Grande Channel to a beach on the southern end of La Caleta. At that point the spit formed a dog-leg, and Carleill landed his men near its joint, at a beach know as La Punta del Judío, now the Playa de Castellgrande. Amazingly, the Spanish had failed to post sentries, relying on mounted patrols and Indian scouts to warn the garrison of any attempt at landing. For some reason the patrols never appeared until it was too late. During the small hours of 10 February almost 1,000 English soldiers and sailors were landed safely, and formed themselves up into attack columns. Drake landed with them, then returned to his ships to organize a naval diversion. Carleill's men made their way up the scrub-covered sand spit without being observed, pausing to avoid the poison-tipped stakes the Spanish had emplaced there to impede progress. As the tide was out they were able to bypass these defences by wading through the surf.

The alarm was raised at around 4.00am, when they were within half a mile of the entrenchments. There La Caleta narrowed to just 150 yards, and spanning it was an earthen wall and parapet, with a ditch in front of it. A battery of four heavy guns covered the approaches, and Carleill could see the two Spanish galleys moving into position to blast him from the flank. Then he spotted the weakness. The Spanish hadn't had time to extend the line of entrenchments beyond the high tide mark on its western or seaward side. After all, they would have found it impossible to dig a trench there. As the tide was out this meant that there was a gap at the end of the Spanish line. The defenders had made a half-hearted attempt to plug it using wine casks filled with sand, but the defences there were unfinished.

Better still for the English, the slight slope of the sand spit meant that the beach was unprotected by the covering fire from the galleys. At least 300 Spanish militia and 200 Indian allies lined the defences, more than one man

Amazingly Drake's landing near Cartagena under cover of darkness was uncontested – and went unreported by enemy scouts. Carleill's assault force then formed into columns and marched up the beach towards their objective. Detail of a coloured engraving by Baptista Boazio.

for each foot of earthen wall. That was when the galleys began to open fire, joined by the defenders of the earthwork. According to Carleill one defender yelled out 'Come on, you heretic dogs', suggesting that at the start of the battle at least, the defenders felt they could hold their assailants at bay. Carleill also noted that the galleys were firing too high, as their shot whistled over the heads of the English troops. That was the moment when he gave the order to charge, yelling 'God and St George!'

His men stormed the seaward end of the defences, jabbing at the defenders with pikes and swords, firing arquebuses and pistols over the makeshift parapet and hauling the wine casks out of the way to create an opening. There was the briefest of fights along the barricade, and then the attackers flooded through the breach. Some of the English columns attacked the earthworks from the flank, rolling up the defences as they went. The rest charged forward over the open ground behind – now La Marina Park – pursuing the defenders, the bulk of whom were now fleeing into the city. Any remaining defenders were cut down where they stood.

Within minutes Carleill and his men were inside the city itself, pursuing the broken defenders through the darkened streets. Don Pedro Fernandez de Busto was inside the city when the English rushed in, and he beat a hasty exit over the San Francisco bridge, accompanied by the remains of his garrison. Only a few pockets of resistance remained. One Spanish captain, Alonso Bravo, stood his ground in the town marketplace in front of the half-built cathedral, but he was forced to surrender after being wounded several times. His men fled. Another knot of defenders tried to rally in front of the bridge, but they were hopelessly outnumbered. Besides, the English manhandled a captured gun forward, and after a few rounds the defenders retired. By dawn, Cartagena was firmly in English hands.

In this early 17th-century engraving, Cartagena is seen from the south, looking over the defences of the Boquerón Channel towards the Inner Harbour. In the far left distance is the spot where Drake's men stormed the city's defences in 1586.

Success on land still left the two galleys defending the Inner Harbour, and Captain Mirabel's garrison of El Boquerón. Don Pedro Vique was on board the *Santiago* when the attack began. He immediately drew in to the beach and landed at the head of a troop of cavalry, carried on board as a mobile striking force. He was unable to prevent the rout, and he and his men were forced back to their boats. Meanwhile, after the collapse of the defences, Captain Castaneda of the *Santiago* tried to support the defenders of the San Francisco bridge by landing troops. Unfortunately, most of his men simply joined the rout, and he was forced to beach his galley under the guns of El Boquerón, and set her on fire. Captain Gonzalez of the *Ocasión* tried to cross the boom and escape into the Outer Harbour, but panic ensued, and after a fire broke out this second galley was also beached beneath El Boquerón. When Don Pedro Vique appeared there was nothing he could do, so he followed his men to safety on the mainland. It would be pleasing to think that those galley slaves who survived were left behind to be captured by the English. More likely they were escorted ashore, and led back into captivity.

The fort of El Boquerón remained defiant. The defences were well sited, and any attempt to approach the fort was met by a barrage of fire. Drake let it be – after all, he had already captured the handful of ships that remained in the Inner Harbour, and the fort was a hindrance rather than a threat. Captain Pedro Mexia Mirabel and his gallant defenders slipped away the following night, which meant that by dawn on 11 February Drake was the undisputed master of Cartagena des Indies, the greatest city on the Spanish Main.

He established his headquarters in the house of the wounded Alonso Bravo, and gathered his commanders to hear their reports. He would have been amazed by what he heard. Christopher Carleill had lost only 28 men, although at least 50 more had been wounded. Spanish losses were even less – a mere nine men – most of who were slain in defence of the makeshift defence on the beach. It has been argued that if the English had been professional soldiers then they would have been defeated. It was the English soldiers' ability to improvise their plan of attack as they went along, and their sheer bravado fuelled by religious animosity and a greed for plunder, that carried them to victory. That, of course, and the leadership of Sir Francis Drake.

Then there came the important business of plunder and ransom. Despite Drake's orders to avoid a looting spree the English soldiers ran amok, ransacking houses and churches until Drake and his officers were able to bring them to heel. Unfortunately for the men, the Spanish had taken all their portable valuables with them before Drake arrived. There was little left to loot. He did capture more than 60 guns, and he immediately ordered his carpenters and gunners to repair their carriages, and to emplace them where they could cover the landward approaches to the city. Drake planned to hold the city until he could negotiate a ransom. He began by demanding ransoms from his prisoners, including his wounded host Alonso Bravo. Drake demanded 5,000 ducats from him to ensure his release, and the sparing of his house and possessions. The two men came to an agreement, and eventually Drake allowed the militia captain to join his wife on the mainland, as she was

OVERLEAF

In February 1586, Sir Francis Drake arrived off Cartagena des Indies, a city known as the 'Jewel of the Spanish Main'. During the early hours of 10 February Drake landed an assault force on a deserted beach on a sand spit, a few miles south of the city. The English soldiers were commanded by Lieutenant-General Christopher Carleill whose men reached the main Spanish defensive line an hour before dawn. These imposing defences spanned a narrow neck of land, but Carleill noticed that it was low tide, and the beach on the Caribbean side of the sand spit was weakly defended – a mere line of sand-filled barrels. He ordered part of his column to 'demonstrate' in front of the main defences, while he led the rest of his troops to the left, towards the shore. When Carleill gave the signal, his assault columns stormed the makeshift barricade. The English outnumbered the defenders, and soon weight of numbers made the difference. When some of the barrels were heaved aside, other soldiers poured through the breach, and within minutes the Spanish defenders were running away, heading into the city, with the English hot on their heels. The fighting only lasted a few ferocious minutes, but with its defences breached and its defenders routed, Cartagena lay at the mercy of Drake and his men.

suffering from fever. When she died Drake allowed her husband to bury her in the city's Franciscan graveyard, and he even attended the funeral, his men firing a volley over the grave as a mark of respect. Drake eventually waived the ransom, and reduced that of the Franciscan priory to a token 600 ducats.

Formal negotiations began on 15 February. Governor Don Pedro Fernandez was summoned to Drake's quarters, accompanied by his leading negotiator Father Don Juan de Montalvo, his deputy governor Don Diego Daca, and Tristan de Oribe Salazar, one of the city's leading merchants. As he had at Santo Domingo, Drake began by demanding a hugely inflated ransom of 400,000 pesos. The Spanish said they were willing to pay up to 25,000. With the negotiations in deadlock, Drake repeated his earlier tactic, and ordered parts of the city to be set on fire. Almost 250 houses were destroyed before the Spanish offered a compromise, and in the end a deal was reached. Drake was offered 107,000 pesos in return for sparing the rest of the city. On top of this, Drake and his men managed to extort all those smaller individual payments, of the kind he had demanded of Alonso Bravo. They amounted to anything up to 250,000 pesos, the majority of which had been gleaned from the Church. He accepted the governor's offer, and for several days mule trains carrying silver and gold kept appearing in the town marketplace, guarded by Carleill and his soldiers.

During these negotiations Drake was both affable and courteous, although Don Pedro Fernandez found him boastful, and prone to launch into bitter tirades aimed at King Philip and Pope Sixtus V. He also bragged about where he might strike next, threatening to attack Panama or Havana, and defeat any Spanish fleet sent to stop him. Drake was certainly thinking about his next move, and clearly the old dream of capturing Nombre de Dios and Panama wasn't far from his mind. He knew he could rely on the Cimaroons as allies, and with the force at his disposal he might have just succeeded. However, events were to overtake him, and would prevent any more major assaults.

By the start of March, the fever that had carried off Alonso Bravo's wife had spread to the city, and during the weeks since its capture more than 100 of Drake's men had died, including his friend George Bonner, captain of the *Bark Bonner*. Incidentally, he also lost another old comrade – Tom Moone, captain of the *Francis*. He had accompanied Drake on his first expedition to the Caribbean, and on his voyage into the Pacific. He and another captain were killed during a skirmish with a small Spanish ship, when it unknowingly sailed into the Outer Harbour. Drake buried his old shipmate in the grounds of Cartagena's cathedral. As March drew to a close and the ransom negotiations were completed, Drake must have been eager to leave. By that stage more than half his men were sick, and the only hope for the remainder was to escape from the festering swamps and dripping humidity of the Venezuelan coast.

Another motivating factor was Cartagena itself. On 27 February, Drake called a Council of War to decide what to do with the city. It was suggested that Cartagena should be held by the English, and turned into a permanent English settlement in the heart of the Spanish New World. While this notion had its attractions, it would have required a monumental effort on the part of the English crown. A fleet would be needed to guarantee its security and supply, and the drain on the Queen's resources would be immense. Besides, with fever spreading rapidly it was clear that Cartagena was hopelessly unhealthy. It was decided to abandon the city as soon as the ransom was collected.

By then it was clear that Drake lacked the manpower to launch another major assault against a Spanish city. That meant he had to abandon his notion of marching across the Isthmus of Panama to assault the city on its Pacific coast. His captains promised to follow him wherever he chose to lead them, but the majority clearly wanted to cut their losses and return home. After all, most of them had joined the expedition purely in the hope of earning a fortune in plunder. While Cartagena had been lucrative, the plunder from the expedition fell far short of what everyone had expected. Eventually, Drake decided to cut his expedition short and return to England. However, he hoped to launch one last assault on the way, ideally against the Cuban capital of Havana, which he discovered was still poorly fortified.

Before they left Cartagena, the English took whatever remaining goods they could, which could be sold for a profit somewhere on the voyage home. It was also claimed that he embarked around 500 slaves, but whether these were given their freedom by Drake is still unclear. As he had Cimaroons in his company, it would have been difficult to treat black slaves as a human commodity. The likelihood is that he planned to transport them to a place of safety. He also took whatever guns he could fit into his ships, leaving Cartagena defenceless. While the official plunder was set at 107,000 pesos, the private plunder brought the total to a more respectable total, possibly as much as 357,000 'pieces-of-eight'. If we add the value of the guns, church bells and other goods, the total increased to more than 500,000 pesos – a respectable haul indeed, and more than Drake's windfall when he captured the *Nuestra Señora del la Concepción* in the Pacific. The only problem was that this time the loot had to be shared between many more people.

Drake finally sailed from the city on 10 April, after spending the best part of two months in Cartagena. Few of his men would have been sad to leave the fever-ridden place. The first attempt to leave was thwarted by a sinking ship. The *New Year Gift,* captured by Drake at Santo Domingo, had begun taking on water soon after she entered the open sea. Drake turned back to repair her, but eventually abandoned the vessel in the Boca Grande anchorage. The extra day was spent baking ship's biscuits, and so it was 12 April before Drake finally disappeared over the horizon. He was only just in time. Two days later a Spanish fleet arrived, sent from Seville to trap Drake. They were too late – El Draque had got clean away.

Behind them the Spanish had to explain the debacle to their King. Don Pedro Fernandez de Busto made a brave start. As he put it: 'I do not know how to begin to tell your Highness of my misfortune... I can only say that it must be God's punishment for my sins, and for those of others.' The worst of it was that the bulk of the official ransom had been paid using royal funds. It would take years for the city to repay the treasury, and to recover from the raid. Meanwhile, its defences had to be rebuilt, its buildings repaired and its citizens had to recover from the traumas of assault, disease and financial ruin. Drake would be remembered for decades to come.

DRAKE'S ASSAULT ON CARTAGENA DES INDIES, TIERRA FIRME

10 FEBRUARY 1586

When Drake arrived off Cartagena des Indies, the city governor was expecting him, and deployed his meagre force to good effect. While his dispositions were good, he had to defend the town and the harbour, and guard against attacks from several directions. By contrast, Drake was able to concentrate his assault force, then unleash it at a key point in the Spanish defences. Once again Drake and his fleet did what they could to distract the defenders, while Robert Carleill and his men delivered the winning blow.

KEY

A English fleet (Drake)

B The English assault force (Carleill) – 1,000 men in 18 companies

C The galleys Santiago and Ocasión (Vique y Manrique) – 300 men

D The Spanish Main defensive line (de Busto) – 500 men, including 200 Indians

E El Boquerón Fort (Mirabel) – 200 men

EVENTS

1 Late on the evening of 9 February, Drake supervises the landing of Carleill and his men on La Punta del Judío, on the southern end of the sand spit of La Caleta. By 2.00am the landing is complete, and Drake returns to the *Elizabeth Bonaventure*.

2 Carleill and his men work their way northwards up La Caleta under cover of darkness. They avoid the poisoned stakes planted to bar their way by bypassing them, wading through the Caribbean surf. Amazingly, no Spanish patrols discover the English assault force.

3 Around 4.00am Carleill is in position, a few hundred yards from the entrenchments spanning the narrow northern neck of La Caleta. At that moment his presence is detected, and the Spanish begin firing on his men from their entrenchments. They are soon joined by the Spanish galleys *Santiago* and *Ocasión* in the Inner Harbour, and by a battery of heavy guns mounted in the centre of the Spanish earthworks.

4 Carleill spots the weakness in the Spanish defence – the earthworks only cover the solid ground of La Caleta, not the beach on the Caribbean side of the line. It is protected by a makeshift barrier of sand-filled barrels. He orders the bulk of his force to storm this barricade, and after a few minutes of fierce hand-to-hand fighting the English column breaks through.

5 The Spanish flee towards the city, pursued by the English soldiers. Within minutes Carleill and his men clamber over the crumbling city wall and enter Cartagena. His men chase the Spaniards through the streets, and although pockets of resistance form at the main square and the bridge leading from the city, these are soon overcome. Cartagena is now in English hands.

6 Meanwhile Drake's fleet 'demonstrates' in front of the Boquerón Channel. The two galleys are unable to escape, and so their commanders beach them beneath El Boquerón fort, and set them on fire. The fort remains in Spanish hands until the following evening. Apart from this last bastion, the 'Jewel of the Spanish Main' falls to Drake.

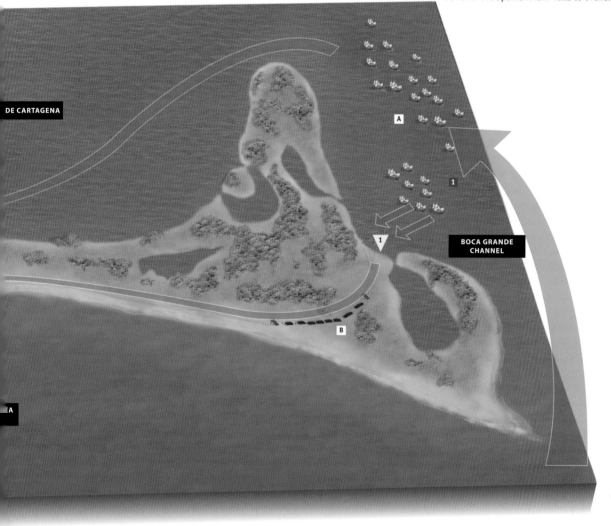

St Augustine

Drake was still eager to attempt two more things before the expedition finally turned for home. First, he wanted to launch a last attack against a Spanish city, preferably Havana. Second, he planned to visit Walter Raleigh's new colony in North America before he began his transatlantic crossing, to see whether it would serve as a useful base for future raids. The fleet headed north, and in late April it entered the Yucatan Channel, between the western tip of Cuba and the Yucatan Peninsula on the Central American coast. Drake may have thought about establishing a settlement on the Cuban coast, using some of his black slaves, freed or otherwise, and a group of freed European galley slaves. He even put into the Cuban mainland somewhere near Cape San Antonio, where he helped his men dig wells in search of fresh water, then helped them carry the filled casks back to the waiting boats. The trouble was, once he rounded the corner of Cuba he was met by a strong south-easterly wind, which made it almost impossible to work his way westwards along the Cuban coast towards Havana. After three weeks Drake gave up the attempt, and headed north, up through the Bahamas Channel.

Drake planned to head straight up the coast of Florida to the English colony on the coast of what is now North Carolina. He could disembark his

The small Spanish colony of St Augustine was attacked by Drake in May 1586. In this engraving by Baptista Boazio the English can be seen using small boats to approach and assault the fort and the defenceless settlement beyond it.

slaves there. The fleet travelled within sight of land, and on 27 May 1586 a lookout spotted a watchtower on the shore, with a small inlet close by. It marked the location of St Augustine, the most northerly town in Spain's New World Empire, and the oldest permanent colonial settlement in North America. Drake had already heard of the place from a Spanish pilot, but he had no idea where it was. Two decades earlier it had served as a base for Pedro Menéndez de Avilés when he attacked and destroyed the nearby French Huguenot settlement of St Caroline. The Spanish then massacred their French prisoners. It therefore gave Drake one final opportunity to raid and plunder, and a chance to avenge his fellow Protestants.

Drake sent a landing party to investigate, while Carleill and a few volunteers rowed a ship's boat into the inlet. The watchtower in the sand dunes was deserted, and there was no sign of any Spaniards. It sat on a strip of sand, separated from the mainland by a band of water, which entered into the inlet. Then they heard the sound of music, a fife. Someone was playing 'William of Nassau', a Protestant song. The musician turned out to be Nicholas Bourgoignon, a French Huguenot who had been taken prisoner by the Spanish six years before, and who now worked as an indentured servant. He agreed to guide the English to the Spanish settlement, which lay on the far side of the water, and just round a bend.

Drake and his men occupied the area of the watchtower, and Carleill and his troops prepared themselves for the coming expedition. Everything seemed peaceful until after midnight, when a sentry fired his arquebus. This was followed by shouts and yells, and the sound of more firing. It was an Indian attack, launched by native allies of the Spanish garrison. Drake and his men held their ground, and the relatively open terrain of the sand dunes worked to their advantage, giving them a reasonable field of fire. Within 20 minutes or so the Indians were repulsed, although it seems the attack was never pressed with much vigour.

The following day, Drake, Carleill and around 200 men advanced up the inlet in pinnaces and small boats, and they soon came across a Spanish stockade fort, Fortaleza Juan, built using upright logs. It was deserted. Inside they found a gun platform with 14 bronze artillery pieces, complete with all their equipment; this powerful battery could have inflicted serious damage on the English boats if the fort had been manned. They also found a chest containing the garrison's pay, about 2,000 gold ducats. What had happened was that Governor Pedro Menéndez Marquez was warned that Drake was off the coast, and he realized that with fewer than 80 militiamen he could offer little in the way of resistance. The garrison and the settlers withdrew inland, leaving Drake to plunder what he could. The chest was probably left behind as an oversight in the rush to quit the settlement. Drake took the guns, and burned the fort to the ground.

A little way beyond the fort the Englishmen came upon St Augustine itself, a forlorn-looking collection of wooden buildings and gardens, capable of housing no more than 300 people. The Spanish were still lingering just beyond the outskirts of the settlement when Drake's men arrived, and they opened up a skirmishing fire. Anthony Powell, one of Carleill's two deputies,

In this stirring painting by the late Angus McBride, Drake is shown rallying his men in the sand dunes outside St Augustine in Florida, when Indians allied to the Spanish launched a surprise night assault on the English camp on the night of 28 May 1586. (Originally in Osprey Elite 70: *Elizabethan Sea Dogs*.)

jumped onto a stray horse and charged the enemy arquebusiers, sword in hand. He was shot from his saddle, then hacked to pieces as he lay wounded. When Carleill and his men arrived, the Spanish melted back into the scrub, leaving Drake in control of the settlement.

The English garrisoned it overnight, then the following morning they collected all tools and implements, anything that would be useful to the settlers, and torched the buildings. Even the orchards and gardens were hacked apart, leaving little of value for the Spanish to return to. Drake's scouts also reported the presence of a nearby Indian village, presumably the home of the warriors who attacked him on the beach. He decided to ignore it, and after a last cast around for plunder, the English returned to their ships.

As a result of the Great Expedition Sir Francis Drake became one of the best-known figures in Europe. Afterwards he led a pre-emptive raid on Cadiz, and commanded part of the English fleet during the Spanish Armada campaign of 1588.

The fleet sailed from St Augustine on 29 May, heading northwards up the coast, looking for signs of Raleigh's settlement. Drake already suspected it lay at a latitude of about 36° North. They looked in to what is now Charleston Harbour, then continued up the coast until they saw smoke. A boat was sent to investigate, and its crew finally made contact with the English settlers, who were encamped on the island of Roanoke, just inside the line of barrier islands now known as the Outer Banks.

It was 9 June. Drake was unable to bring his fleet through the Outer Banks, so he dropped anchor, and accompanied a flotilla of smaller boats as they sailed through the inlet to Roanoke. On the island Drake met Ralph Lane, the governor of the settlement. It was clear that the settlement wasn't prospering, so Drake made Lane an offer – take passage back to England with him, or remain where he was, in which case Drake would give him whatever supplies he needed. Lane bravely elected to stay where he was, and so Drake's men ferried provisions and tools from the fleet to the settlement. For the most part Lane's men were soldiers rather than farmers, and therefore they lacked the skills needed to plant a sustainable crop. Drake did what he could, and left them a small ship – the *Francis* – and a pinnace which they could use to fish from, together with a handful of volunteer seamen to crew the vessels.

While Drake was busy on Roanoke a storm hit the coast, and the ships had no option but to work their way out to sea, rather than try to ride out the storm at anchor off a lee shore. By the time the storm passed several of the ships had been scattered, including the *Sea Dragon*, *Talbot*, *White Lion* and the *Francis* – the ship earmarked for the colony. Most of these vessels made their own way back to England.

With the *Francis* gone, Drake offered Lane a replacement – the *Bark Bonner* – and fresh provisions. However, by that stage the colonists had undergone a change of heart, and they begged Drake to take them with him. Consequently the settlement was abandoned, and on 18 June Drake set sail, bound for England. Ironically, less than a week later Sir Ralph Grenville arrived with more colonists and a years' worth of supplies. He left the fresh colonists and supplies on the island and returned home, sailing about two weeks behind Drake and his fleet. The new colonists fared even worse than their predecessors. By the time fresh supplies were brought out the following year, there was no trace of either the colonists or the colony. What happened to these pioneers remains one of the longest-standing mysteries in colonial American history.

At first Drake hoped to continue his voyage northwards, as he planned to raid the Spanish fishing stations around Labrador and Newfoundland. He was thwarted by contrary winds, however, and so he reluctantly set a course for home. On 27 July 1586, Drake and the remains of his expedition sailed into Plymouth, where they were met by cheering crowds lining the quayside. The great expedition had lasted ten months, and cost the lives of hundreds of Englishmen. In return, a fair amount of plunder had been obtained, but far more importantly Spain had been humbled. This then was Drake's achievement. Diplomatically the raid failed to stop King Philip from beginning a war with England – in fact, it probably made such a war inevitable. What it did achieve, though, was to shatter the illusion that the Spanish were a great power. Drake had pillaged four Spanish settlements with ease, and demonstrated the vulnerability of the Spanish overseas empire. Just as importantly, with war looming, the English now believed they could take on the might of Spain and win.

COUNTING THE COST

Was Drake's great expedition a success? Did it achieve its objectives? One of the problems with arriving at a judgement is that its success was measured by two groups – the investors and the Queen's policy advisors. To confuse matters further, for the most part these appear to have been the same people. Drake had set out to cause serious damage to Spanish interests in the New World, humiliate Philip II of Spain by demonstrating his inability to defend his realm and divert the annual flow of New World silver and gold from the Spanish treasury to the English coffers. The other objective was to make as much money for his investors as he could, a difficult task given the high cost of fitting out the expedition (placed at around £60,000–70,000) and the substantial number of people who expected to profit from the enterprise. This was the problem with Elizabethan expeditions of this kind: they were joint-stock ventures as well as state-sponsored privateering raids. The two elements – national policy and financial investment – were not necessarily complementary. Drake was therefore torn between hurting the Spanish and turning a profit.

England's profit

Financially, the expedition was not a great success. The exact value of the plunder Drake brought home is unclear, largely because his accountant died of disease during the voyage, and Drake lacked the clerical abilities to put the books in order before he returned home. We can assume that Drake gained 82,000 pesos from Santo Domingo (a combination of ransom and plunder). A further 357,000 pesos of ransom was extorted from the citizens of Cartagena and the city governor. A meagre 4,000 pesos were recovered from St Augustine, which brings the total haul to 443,000 pesos. That represents the equivalent of 221,500 gold ducats, which were roughly the same as the English pound. Even if we reduce the total slightly due to vagaries in conversion rates, gold or silver quality and the contemporary devaluation of Spanish silver, this still means that Drake's haul was probably something in the region of £200,000.

On top of that there was the value of the goods taken from Cartagena – the bronze guns, church bells and other portable items. That probably amounted to another 140,000 pesos – the equivalent of £60,000. On Drake's return a committee was formed, and an audit held. After much deliberation, its chairman Sir William Wynter announced that the total proceeds amounted to just £65,000. Before that, though, those who took part in the expedition were awarded their share of the plunder. We know that Drake applied to the committee for the money he needed to pay off his men. There were also accusations that Drake kept an undue share of the profits for himself, and that the plunder was partially divided long before the fleet arrived back in Plymouth.

The truth, of course, will probably never be known. All the investors, including Queen Elizabeth, received an initial return on their investment of just 75 per cent, which means they made a loss. Drake would have been concerned about this, as given the way these ventures operated, without more financial backers he wouldn't be able to command any more expeditions. He even waived the right to recoup his own quite considerable costs in fitting out the expedition, which increased the return for his other backers. However, what this official figure doesn't take into account is the value of the goods that had to be sold, all of which would generate additional income, and which was earmarked for the pockets of the investors. Even if the goods were sold for half their estimated value, that would still generate another £30,000, more than enough to pay off the investors and return them a reasonable but unspectacular profit.

By all estimates, that still left something in the region of £150,000. Most of this would have been earmarked as prize money, to be divided amongst the crew. Although no records survive of Drake's expedition, we can draw on other contemporary examples to see how prize money was allocated. A set proportion of the plunder – often as much as three-fifths – would be allocated as prize money, and the rest earmarked for the financial backers. We don't know the exact percentage used to determine the allocation on Drake's expedition, but around 30–50 per cent would have been normal as prize money. This allocation was fair enough; after all, these were the men who bled and suffered for the money. In some cases, a deduction would be made as recompense to the dead or injured. The allocation on behalf of the 700 or so men who perished during the expedition would be earmarked for their relatives if any had been registered before the fleet sailed, or else returned to the common fund. The wounded often received a bonus, in proportion to the severity of their injuries.

Whatever was left would be divided up amongst the crew. A sliding scale was used, with captains receiving a greater portion than other ship's officers, and seamen with specific skills earning more than ordinary seamen. For instance, a captain could receive 2 shares, an officer 1½ and a seaman 1. Drake of course would earn the highest proportion of all. It was later claimed that the return for an ordinary soldier or sailor who took part in the expedition was £6. This seems especially low, the equivalent of a year's wages for an Elizabethan sailor. Even if we set aside larger portions for the dead and bonus payments for the wounded, it still comes to little more than about £20,000.

That still left the best part of £100,000 unaccounted for. While some historians have argued that Drake probably secreted the money away for himself, the truth is he would have found this almost impossible to do. His men had a stake in the profits, and would have been too vigilant. Another possibility – that it was given to the crown as part of a pre-arranged deal – isn't borne out by the royal accounts, as the money never showed up on the books. Rumours persisted that Drake sent Robert Dudley, Earl of Leicester, a payment of 50,000 ducats, the rough equivalent of £50,000, but this was never been proven. Then again, at the time Leicester was busy

While silver mining was important, the prosperity of Spain's settlements on the Spanish Main was largely dependent on crop production and slave labour. This late 16th-century depiction of a Spanish sugar plantation was engraved by Theodore de Bry.

raising an English army to fight alongside the Dutch rebels. This might well have been the kind of secretive payment Elizabeth's spymaster Francis Walsingham might have arranged.

Others have pointed out that these men were angrily petitioning Wynter's committee, demanding their money, which suggests nobody – not even Drake – had received their prize money until a month after the expedition returned home. This situation suggests that there was no initial distribution at sea – a common practice during the period – which would have given the sailors spending money to hand before they reached Plymouth. If this was done then the sums involved were so low that the men spent their extra bounty within days of their arrival, not an impossible feat for a sailor denied the pleasures of home for so long.

Such early payments still wouldn't have accounted for more than a tiny fraction of the missing £100,000. A more likely explanation is that it never existed, and the estimates of plunder recovered from Cartagena were hopelessly exaggerated. The Spanish themselves claimed that the money and goods taken by Drake and his men were valued at 400,000 pesos. They might well have been exaggerating wildly, in the hope of recompense from the Spanish crown. This interpretation is reinforced by the general impression that the expedition was a financial failure. After all, if Drake had that much plunder left over, a mere quarter of it would have been enough to ensure all the investors revived a profitable return on their investment in the initial division. Unhappy investors meant less chance anyone would put up the money for another expedition. The most likely explanation remains that the haul of plunder was overvalued. Of course, even though this means the expedition was less than successful, there was also that other criterion for success – the political one.

Spain's loss

When Drake returned home, one of the first things he did was to write to William Cecil, Lord Burghley. Not only was he one of Drake's leading backers, but he was also the Lord High Treasurer, and one of Queen Elizabeth's closest advisors. Drake began by hoping that the voyage would be the foundation for even greater ventures. He continued: 'My very good Lord, there is now a very wide gap opened, very little to the liking of the King of Spain. God work it all to his glory.' He meant that he had exposed the greatest weakness of King Philip's Spain, alluding to the fact that the treasure ports of the Spanish Main lay open to attack. Spanish military and naval power depended on the flow of gold and silver from the New World to Spain. Drake now reckoned that the English could render Spain militarily impotent by intercepting these treasure shipments, capturing Spanish treasure ports and generally destroying Spain's infrastructure in her overseas empire.

Lord Burghley was well aware that the raid had proved a major humiliation for the Spanish. It was no exaggeration when in a letter to the Queen he declared that 'Sir Francis Drake is a man fearful to the King of Spain'. He was right. The capture of Santo Domingo and Cartagena – two key cities in the Spanish New World – demonstrated to the international powers just how vulnerable King Philip's empire actually was. The message was certainly understood by Spain's creditors – within months of Drake's return King Philip was turned down for a loan of 500,000 ducats, one supplied jointly by the Papacy and the Florentine banks. The banking house in Seville collapsed as rumours spread throughout Europe that the Spanish couldn't safeguard their annual shipments of treasure. Even Pope Sixtus V admitted that Drake's achievements had been impressive. Politically, the raid was a resounding success.

Just as importantly, the Spanish had no idea when and where Drake would strike next. Sir Francis had become one of the most talked-about men in Europe, and in 1586 England had a national hero who seemed capable of achieving anything he wanted. The boost to national morale was incalculable. As the prospects of war loomed ever larger, at least England could count on men like Sir Francis Drake to protect them from the wrath of the Spanish. The irony, of course, is that if anyone helped bring about this war, it was Drake himself, as by now King Philip realized that he could only safeguard his empire by destroying Queen Elizabeth's England.

CONCLUSION

With the benefit of hindsight we can see that the belief that Drake's raid would help prevent a war was incredibly naive. The idea was that it would give King Philip pause, and make him consider the consequences of an all-out war with England. Of course, Drake's raid achieved exactly the opposite. At the time King Philip was embroiled in a long and costly war against the Dutch Protestant rebels. His commander, the Duke of Parma, captured the city of Antwerp in August 1585, which safeguarded Spain's earlier conquests in the Spanish Netherlands. He was irritated by overt English support for the rebels, and so before launching a final offensive against the Dutch, King Philip felt he needed to deal with the English problem once and for all. That effectively meant invading England.

The unusual location of England's first New World colony is clearly seen in this engraving by Theodore de Bry. Roanoke Island is protected from the Atlantic by a chain of barrier islands, and could only be reached by small boat.

Back in Spain, King Philip's advisors argued that Drake's success would encourage others, and the seas would be filled by English privateers, all eager for a share of Spain's riches. The first of these privateers were already at sea. Only by defeating England could Spanish sea communications be protected, and the security of her overseas empire preserved. Consequently King Philip asked his leading commanders, the Duke of Santa Cruz and the Duke of Parma, to draft plans for an invasion. This set in train the events which would lead to Spain's 'Great Enterprise against England' – the Spanish Armada of 1588.

Drake's assault on Cartagena, as depicted in the engraving by Baptista Boazio in 1588. As in his other maps, Boazio shows several actions at the one moment, including the probing of the harbour, Drake's amphibious landing and Carleill's dawn assault.

When the Spanish Armada appeared, Sir Francis Drake played a not insignificant part in the fighting, as did many of the ships and men who accompanied him to the Caribbean. However, the Spanish Armada was defeated as much by luck as naval prowess, a combination of contrary winds, unfavourable tides and unseasonable gales all played their part in thwarting King Philip's great invasion force. Although the war would drag on after the death of both Elizabeth and Philip, neither side achieved a decisive victory. Other expeditions would be launched against the Spanish overseas empire, but none achieved the success of Drake's great expedition of 1585–86. For their part the Spanish learned their lesson, and not only fortified their treasure ports, but they now provided their treasure ships with powerful escorts. Drake's raid proved to be the last of its kind. The ageing Drake and Hawkins would both succumb to disease during a last raid on the Spanish Main in 1595–96, and their deaths marked the passing of an era – the age of the Elizabethan Sea Dogs.

FURTHER READING

Andrews, Kenneth R., *Elizabethan Privateering*, Cambridge University Press, Cambridge (1964)

Apestegui, Cruz, *Pirates of the Caribbean: Buccaneers, Privateers, Freebooters and Filibusters, 1493–1720*, Conway Maritime Press, London (2002)

Bawlf, Samuel, *The Secret Voyage of Sir Francis Drake*, Penguin, London (2004)

Chartrand, René, *The Spanish Main, 1492–1800*, Osprey Publishing, Oxford (2006)

Cummins, John, *Francis Drake*, Weidenfeld & Nicolson, London (1997)

Davis, Ralph, *The Rise of the Atlantic Economies*, Weidenfeld & Nicolson, London (1982)

Dudley, Wade, *Drake: For God, Queen and Plunder*, Brassey's US /Potomac Books, Dulles, VA (2003)

Kelsey, Harry, *Sir Francis Drake: The Queen's Pirate*, Yale University Press, New Haven, CT (2000)

Kelsey, Harry, *Sir John Hawkins: Queen Elizabeth's Slave Trader*, Yale University Press, New Haven, CT (2003)

Konstam, Angus, *Elizabethan Sea Dogs, 1560–1605*, Osprey Publishing, Oxford (2008)

Konstam, Angus, *Piracy: the Complete History*, Osprey Publishing, Oxford (2008)

Konstam, Angus, *Tudor Warships (2): Elizabeth I's Navy*, Osprey Publishing, Oxford (2008)

Konstam, Angus, *The World Atlas of Pirates*, Lyons Press, New York, NY (2009)

Milton, Giles, *Big Chief Elizabeth: How England's Adventurers Gambled and Won the New World*, Hodder & Stoughton, London (2000)

Nelson, Arthur, *The Tudor Navy: The Ships, Men and Organisation, 1485–1603*, Conway Maritime Press, London (2001)

Parry, J.H., *The Spanish Seaborne Empire*, Hutchinson, London (1966)

Roche, T.W.E., *The Golden Hind*, Arthur Baker Ltd, London (1973)

Ronald, Susan, *The Pirate Queen: Queen Elizabeth I, Her Pirate Adventurers, and the Dawn of Empire*, Harper Collins, London (2009)

Starkey, David, *Elizabeth I*, Vintage, London (2001)

Sugden, John, *Sir Francis Drake*, Touchstone, New York, NY (1990)

Thompson, George Malcolm, *Sir Francis Drake*, Secker & Warburg Ltd, London (1973)

Wagner, Henry R., *Sir Francis Drake's Voyage Round the World*, N. Israel, Amsterdam (1969)

Walton, Timothy, *The Spanish Treasure Fleets*, Pineapple Press, Sarasota, FL (1994)

Williams, Neville, *Francis Drake*, Weidenfeld & Nicolson, London (1973)

Williamson, James A., *The Age of Drake*, Adam & Charles Black, London (1965)

INDEX

DISCARD